Beyond the Baker's Basics

Advanced Dessert Delicacies

By

Christina P. Tilton

DESSERTS.

Directions for preparing all kinds of desserts, cold and warm; puddings, puff pastes, souffles, sherbets, creams, ices and ice creams.

Steamed Puddings.

No. 1—RICE PUDDING.

Quantity for 6 Persons.

½ lb. of rice
1 qt. of milk
¼ lb. of fresh butter
¼ lb. of sugar, scant
¼ lb. of raisins
¼ lb. of ground almonds
7 eggs
1 pinch of salt

Preparation: The rice is washed and brought to boil in 1 cup of water. When the water is boiled down, add the milk gradually and 1 pinch of salt and boil to a thick mush. When done, cool it off. Cream the butter, add sugar, 7 yolks of eggs, raisins, almonds and the beaten whites of eggs. Butter a pudding mold, strew in some bread crumbs, put in the rice pudding, close the mold well and set in a steamer over a kettle of boiling water and boil for 1½ hours. When serving, turn the pudding out on a platter and serve cold with a vanilla or wine sauce or sweet cream.

No. 2—APPLE RICE PUDDING.

Quantity for 6 Persons.

½ lb. of rice
¾ qt. of milk
⅛ lb. of butter
¼ lb. of raisins
7 eggs
1 pinch of salt
6 sweet-sour apples
1 cup of sugar
¼ lb. of blanched, ground almonds

Preparation: The rice is cooked slowly with one cup of water; when the water is boiled down, add the milk gradually and cook it to a thick mush. Cream the butter, add the sugar, then the yolks of eggs, raisins and almonds. Let rice cool, then mix all together. The apples are peeled, cored, cut into 16 parts and stewed until tender in a little water and sugar. Butter a pudding mold and strew with bread crumbs. Stir the well-beaten whites of the 7 eggs into the rice, put a layer of rice into the mold, then a layer of apples and repeat this twice; the last layer to be rice. Close the mold, set in a steamer over a kettle of boiling water and boil 1½ hours, then turn over on platter and serve with sweet cream.

No.3—CHERR YRICEPUDDING.

Quantity for 6 Persons.

½ lb. of rice
¾ qts. of milk
⅛ lb. butter
7 eggs
¼ lb. of peeled and ground almonds
¼ lb. of raisins
1 lb. stoned sour cherries
1 cup of sugar

Preparation: The preparation is again the same as No. 2, instead of apples put in layers of sour cherries, boiled until tender in 1 cup of sugar and 1 cup of water. Boil down the cherry juice with sugar to taste and serve it with the pudding.

No.4—PEACHRICEPUDDING.

Quantity for 6 Persons.

½ lb. of rice
¾ qt. of milk
7 eggs
⅛ lb. of butter
¼ lb. of peeled and ground almonds
¼ lb. of raisins
1½ lbs. of peaches
½ lb. of sugar

Preparation: The preparation is again the same as No. 2, instead of apples put in layers of peaches, boiled until tender in 1 cup of water and one of sugar. Boil down the peach juice, putting in a few stones which should be removed before serving, and serve the syrup with the pudding.

No.5—APRICOTRICEPUDDING.

Quantity for 6 Persons.

½ lb. of rice
¾ qt. of milk
⅛ lb. of butter
7 eggs
1½ lbs. of stoned apricots
¼ lb. of sugar
¼ lb. of peeled and ground almonds
¼ lb. of raisins

Preparation: The preparation is the same as given under No. 2, see Apple Rice Pudding. Instead of apples put in layers of apricots boiled until tender in 1 cup of water and ½ cup of sugar. Boil down the juice with some sugar and serve with the pudding.

No.6—PLAINRICEPUDDING.

Quantity for 6 Persons.

½ lb. of rice
1 qt. of milk
¼ lb. of butter
7 eggs
¼ lb. of sugar

Preparation: The preparation is the same as given under No. 1, Rice Pudding.

No.7—FROTHORFOAMPUDDING.

Quantity for 6 Persons.

½ pt. of milk
¼ lb. of butter
¼ lb. of sugar
¼ lb. of fine flour
1 lemon peel
8 eggs

Preparation: The milk is brought to boil, the butter added, sugar and flour are mixed and stirred into the boiling milk until the mixture comes off the sides of the skillet. Then cool it, grate the lemon peel and stir it in with the yolks of eggs and the beaten whites. Butter a pudding mold and strew in bread crumbs, then put in the pudding, set in a steamer over a kettle of boiling water, cover the mold tightly and boil for 2 hours. Turn it, and serve with a fruit sauce.

No.8—CABINETPUDDING.

Quantity for 6 Persons.

8 zwieback
12 lady fingers
¼ lb. of raisins
¼ lb. of currants
1 pt. of milk
1 pt. of cream
6 eggs
¼ lb. of sugar

Preparation: The zwieback is broken into 3 parts, the lady fingers into halves. Butter a mold and make a layer of zwieback, raisins, currants, then one of lady fingers, repeat this 2 to 3 times, the last layer being zwieback. Then mix well the milk, cream, sugar and eggs and pour on the pudding, set in a steamer over a kettle of boiling water and boil 1½ hours. When done, turn it out on a platter and serve with a wine sauce.

No.9—WHEA TBREADPUDDING.

Quantity for 6 Persons.

¼ lb. of fresh butter
6 eggs
¼ lb. of sugar
½ cup of raisins
¼ cup of currants
½ cup of fine cut citron
½ cup blanched, grated almonds
4 milk rolls

Preparation: Cream, the butter with yolks of eggs, sugar, raisins, currants, citron and almonds, mix and stir well. The crust of the rolls is grated off, then they are soaked in milk, the surplus milk pressed out and the rolls stirred with the rest of the ingredients, also the beaten whites of eggs. Butter a mold, strew with bread crumbs, put in the pudding and steam 1 hour. Serve with a fruit sauce.

No.10—PLUMPUDDING.

Quantity for 6–8 Persons.

1 pinch of salt
1 lb. raisins
1 lb. currants
1 lb. of flour
1 lb. of sugar
1 lb. beef kidney suet
6 eggs
1 lemon peel
2 cups of milk
2 small cups of grated bread
½ cup of brandy
Rum

Preparation: Raisins and currants are washed well and dried. The suet is chopped very fine and mixed well with 6 eggs, sugar, raisins, currants, grated lemon peel, milk, bread crumbs, brandy and lastly the flour. Butter a mold, strew with bread crumbs, put in the pudding and steam for 5 hours. Turn the pudding out on a platter, pour the rum over and light it. The flaming pudding is brought to the table and served with a wine sauce.

No.11—CHOCOLATEPUDDING.

Quantity for 6 Persons.

1 pt. of milk
Scant ¼ lb. of butter
¼ lb. grated sweet chocolate
Scant ¼ lb. of sugar
⅛ lb. blanched, ground almonds
6 eggs
¼ lb. fine flour

Preparation: The milk is brought to boil, butter, sugar, flour, chocolate well stirred in until the mixture comes off the sides of the skillet, then take from the stove. Cool it and stir in the almonds, yolks of eggs and the beaten whites.

Butter a mold, strew with bread crumbs, fill with the pudding, cover tightly and steam 1½ hours, then turn out on a platter and serve with a vanilla sauce.

Remarks: The dish must be only ¾ full because the pudding raises very much.

No.12—FLOURPUDDING.

Quantity for 6 Persons.

¼ lb. of fine flour
8 eggs
½ grated lemon peel
¼ lb. of sugar
4 tbsps. of lemon juice

Preparation: Beat the yolks of eggs with sugar 20 minutes, add lemon juice and grated rind and lastly stir in the flour, which must be sifted 4 times. The whites of eggs are beaten to a stiff froth and mixed in. Butter a mold, put in the pudding, close it well and steam 1¼ hours. Turn the pudding on a platter and serve with a wine sauce.

No.13—LAYERPUDDING.

Quantity for 6 Persons.

½ pt. of cream
¼ lb. of flour
⅛ lb. of butter
5 beaten whites of eggs
¼ lb. of sugar
½ lemon peel
5 yolks of eggs

FortheFilling.

½ lb. peach marmalade, or 1 qt. of cherry or strawberry preserves

ForBetweenLayers,4SmallPancakes.

¼ lb. of flour
3 tbsps. of butter
4 eggs
1 pinch of salt
¼ lemon peel
Butter, for baking
¼ pt. of milk

Preparation: Cream, flour, butter, yolks of eggs are mixed well and brought to boil. When the batter rolls from the sides of the pot, take it off the fire to cool. Then add sugar, grated lemon peel, and 5 whites of eggs beaten to a stiff froth.

Now bake the pancakes. Mix well the milk, flour, 3 tablespoonfuls of melted butter, 4 eggs and a little salt. Heat a pan with butter and bake the pancakes the size of the pudding dish. Now butter the mold, strew bread crumbs in, make 1 layer of pudding batter, one layer of fruit marmalade or preserved fruit as peaches, cherries, strawberries or raspberries; on this fruit layer, place a pancake, then another layer of pudding batter, again a layer of fruit, another pancake and so on according to the number of pancakes you have. The top layer must be the pudding batter. Close the dish well and steam for 1½ hours. When done, turn the pudding out and serve with a fruit sauce.

No.14—FARINA PUDDING No.1.

Quantity for 6 Persons.

1 pt. of milk
1 cup of fine farina
⅛ lb. of butter
Scant ¼ lb. of sugar
¼ lb. of blanched, ground almonds
The rind of ¼ lemon
6 eggs

Preparation: Milk and butter are brought to boil, the farina stirred in, the sugar and lemon rind added and all stirred and cooked until the batter rolls from the sides of the skillet, then cool it off and add almonds, yolks of eggs and beaten whites. Butter a mold, strew with roll crumbs, put in the pudding, close the mold well and steam 1½ hours. Turn the pudding out on a platter and serve with cherry or raspberry sauce.

No.15—MACARONI PUDDING.

Quantity for 6 Persons.

Ingredients and preparation are the same as given under No. 56, in Chapter 15, Macaroni Pudding.

No.16—POTATO PUDDING.

Quantity for 6 Persons.

Ingredients and preparation are given in Chapter 11, No. 16, Potato Pudding.

No. 17—MEAT PUDDING WITH RICE LAYERS.

Quantity for 6 Persons.

Ingredients, and preparation are the same as given as in Chapter 2, Beef, No. 2, Meat Pudding, from Roast Beef, Stew or Soup Meat.

No. 18—ANOTHER FORM OF MEAT PUDDING.

Quantity for 6 Persons.

Ingredients and preparation are the same as given in Chapter 2, Beef, No. 26, Meat Pudding.

No. 19—MUTTON KIDNEY PUDDING.

Quantity for 6 Persons.

Ingredients and preparations are given in Chapter 4, Lamb, No. 20, Lamb Kidney Pudding.

No. 20—VEAL ROAST PUDDING.

Quantity for 6 Persons.

Ingredients and preparation are the same as given in Chapter 3, Veal, No. 6, Veal Roast Pudding.

No. 21—GOOSE LIVER PUDDING.

Quantity for 6 Persons.

Ingredients and preparation are given in Chapter 6, Poultry, No. 26, Goose Liver Pudding.

No.22—CHERRY PUDDING.

Quantity for 6–8 Persons.

8 milk rolls
¾ qt. of milk
¼ lb. of butter
8 eggs
Rind of 1 lemon
¼ tsp. of cinnamon
2 lbs. stoned cherries
¾ cup of sugar

Preparation: The milk rolls are grated and soaked in milk. When well soaked, press out the milk and rub them through a strainer or colander. Melt the butter in a spider, put in the mashed rolls and sauté or dry fry them on the stove. Now mix this well with yolks of eggs, grated lemon rind, cinnamon, sugar, stoned cherries and cherry syrup. Beat the whites of eggs to a stiff froth and add to the mixture. Butter a pudding mold, strew in bread crumbs, then fill with the pudding and steam for 2 hours. Turn out and serve.

No.23—FARINA PUDDING No.2.

Quantity for 6 Persons.

1 qt. of milk
¼ lb. of butter
¾ cup of sugar
1 grated lemon peel
¾ cup of fine farina
8 bitter almonds
¼ lb. sweet almonds
8 eggs

Preparation: The milk and butter are brought to boil, then the sugar, lemon peel and farina poured in and cooked 5 minutes to a thick paste, stirring constantly. Now take from the fire, cool off and add blanched and ground sweet and bitter almonds, the 8 yolks of eggs and the beaten whites. Butter a pudding mold, strew with bread crumbs, put in the pudding and steam 1½ hours. Turn the pudding out and serve with a fruit or wine sauce.

No.24—SOURCREAMPUDDING.

Quantity for 6 Persons.

½ pt. thick, sour cream
Juice and peel of ½ lemon
10 eggs 1 cup of currants
¾ lb. of roll crumbs
¼ tsp. of salt
¼ cup of sugar

Preparation: The thick sour cream is mixed well and stirred 10 minutes with juice and grated peel of lemon, yolks of eggs, roll crumbs, salt, currants and beaten whites of eggs. A mold is buttered and strewn with roll crumbs, the pudding filled in and steamed 1½ hours. Then it is turned out on a platter and served with a wine or fruit sauce.

No.25—BLACKPUDDING.

Quantity for 6 Persons.

½ lb. of ground almonds
¼ lb. sweet chocolate
¼ lb. of sugar
⅛ lb. of small raisins
¼ cup chopped citron
¼ tsp. cinnamon
⅛ tsp. ground cloves
¾ cup of roll crumbs
¼ cup of white wine

6 eggs

Preparation: The unblanched almonds are ground, the chocolate grated. Sugar and yolks of eggs are stirred 20 minutes, then mixed well with almonds, chocolate, raisins, citron, cinnamon, cloves, roll crumbs, white wine and beaten whites of eggs. Butter a mold, strew it with crumbs, put in the pudding, close it well and steam 1½ hours. Turn it out and serve with a chocolate sauce.

No.26—PUDDING A LA BRANDENBURG.

Quantity for 6–8 Persons.

1 pt. of milk
⅛ lb. of butter
¼ lb. flour, good measure
¼ lb. of sugar
⅛ lb. of blanched, chopped sweet almonds
1 tbsp. chopped bitter almonds
2 tbsps. chopped citron
1 tbsp. chopped orange rind
½ grated lemon peel
7 eggs
¼ cup of rum

Preparation: Milk and butter are brought to boil, add the flour and boil, stirring constantly till it comes from the sides of the skillet. Cool and stir in the sugar, sweet and bitter almonds, citron, orange and lemon peel, yolks of eggs and the beaten whites. Butter a pudding mold, strew it with roll crumbs, put in the pudding, close well and steam for 2 hours. Turn the pudding out on a platter, pour on ¼ cup of rum, light it and bring it to the table. Serve with a wine sauce.

Warm Puddings, Baked Puddings.

No.27—BAKED CREAM PUDDING.

Quantity for 6 Persons.

¾ qt. of sour cream
¾ cup of sugar
½ lemon peel
2 tbsps. of lemon juice
3 tbsps. of flour
7 eggs

Preparation: The sour cream is mixed well with sugar, grated lemon peel, lemon juice, flour, 7 yolks of eggs and beaten whites. Then bake in the oven in a buttered pudding dish for 25 to 30 minutes.

No.28—BAKED RICE PUDDING.

Quantity for 6 Persons.

1 cup of rice
¾ qt. of milk
⅛ lb. of butter
4 eggs
½ cup of sugar

Preparation: The rice is boiled to a thick mush with milk. Cream the butter with sugar and yolks of eggs, add the rice and the beaten whites of eggs, fill into a buttered pudding dish and bake in oven ½ hour.

Remarks: The pudding may be made richer with ¼ lb. blanched, ground almonds, ½ cup of raisins, 6 to 8 eggs instead of 4.

No.29—BAKED RICE PUDDING WITH FRUIT LAYERS.

Quantity for 6 Persons.

1 cup of rice
¾ qt. of milk
⅛ lb. of butter
1 qt. boiled fruit, (cherries, apricots or peaches)
6 eggs
½ cup of sugar

Preparation: The preparation of the rice is the same as given under No. 28, Baked Rice Pudding.

The buttered pudding dish is filled with alternating layers of rice and fruit, from which the juice has been drained. Put in 3 layers of each and the top layer should be rice. Bake in oven for 1 hour and serve with the sauce from the fruit used in the pudding.

No.30—BAKEDF ARINAPUDDINGWITHFRUIT .

Quantity for 6 Persons.

1 qt. of milk
1 cup of farina
¼ lb. of butter
1 grated lemon rind
3 tbsps. of lemon juice
¼ lb. sugar
5 eggs
1 qt. cherries

Preparation: The milk is brought to boil, the farina put in and stirred 10 minutes. Let it get cold. Cream the butter, add grated lemon rind, lemon juice, sugar, 5 yolks of eggs and the farina and stir in the beaten whites of eggs. Butter a pudding dish and fill it with alternating layers of farina and cherries, 2 layers of each; the top layer should be farina. Put a few pieces of butter over the top and bake in oven 1 hour.

No.31—BAKED CHERRY PUDDING.

Quantity for 6 Persons.

¼ lb. of butter
¼ lb. of sugar
6 eggs
¼ lb. blanched, ground almonds
3 rolls
3 lbs. sweet cherries

Preparation: Soak the rolls in milk, cream the butter with sugar, add the yolks of eggs, almonds and rolls, after pressing out the milk; mix well, add the stoned cherries and beaten whites of eggs. Butter a baking dish, put in the pudding and bake in oven 1 hour.

No.32—BAKED LEMON PUDDING.

Quantity for 6 Persons.

8 eggs
¼ lb. of sugar
½ lemon peel
1 tbsp. corn starch
Juice of 1½ lemons

Preparation: The 8 yolks of eggs are beaten ¼ hour with sugar, lemon juice and grated lemon peel, the corn starch and beaten whites of eggs added last. Butter a baking dish, fill in the pudding and bake 15 minutes.

No.33—BAKED POTATO PUDDING.

Quantity for 6 Persons.

½ lb. boiled, grated potatoes
6 eggs

½ pt. of cream
¼ lb. of sugar
1 grated lemon rind

Preparation: Cream the yolks of eggs and sugar, add the grated lemon peel, grated potatoes, cream, beaten whites of eggs, and mix well. Put the batter into a buttered baking dish and bake in oven 45 minutes. Serve with a fruit sauce.

No.34—BAKEDPOT ATOPUDDING.

To be Served with Meat.

Quantity for 6 Persons.

8 medium-sized potatoes
1/10 lb. of butter
2–3 eggs
½ tbsp. Parmesan cheese
1 pinch of pepper
Salt to taste

Preparation: The potatoes are boiled, peeled and grated. Cream the butter with the yolks of eggs, add the potatoes, cheese, salt, pepper and beaten whites of eggs. Butter a casserole or pudding dish, put the pudding in, sprinkle bread crumbs and pieces of butter over the top and bake in oven 45 minutes.

No.35—BAKEDCHARLOTTEPUDDING.

Quantity for 6 Persons.

6 rolls
½ pt. of milk almonds
¼ pt. of white wine
¼ lb. of sugar

½ cup of blanched, ground
½ cup of raisins
½ grated lemon peel
4 eggs

Preparation: The rolls are soaked in milk and wine, add ground almonds, sugar, raisins, lemon peel, yolks of 4 eggs and lastly the beaten whites of eggs. A baking dish is buttered, the pudding filled in and baked in oven 45 minutes. A fruit or wine sauce is served with the pudding.

No.36—BAKED ALMOND PUDDING.

Quantity for 6 Persons.

8 eggs
¼ lb. blanched, ground almonds
¾ cup of sugar
¼ lb. fine flour

Preparation: The yolks of eggs, almonds and sugar are stirred 20 minutes, then the flour and whites of eggs added. A pudding dish is buttered, the pudding filled in and baked 45 minutes.

No.37—BAKED YORKSHIRE PUDDING.

Quantity for 6 Persons.

1 egg
1 white of egg
½ pt. of milk
1 pinch of salt
6 tbsps. of butter
6 tbsps. of mutton suet
1 cup of flour

Preparation: Egg, white of egg, milk and flour are mixed well. Butter is heated in a pudding dish, the batter put in, the suet heated and poured over and the pudding baked in a hot oven 20 minutes.

No.38—BAKEDCHOCOLA TEPUDDING.

Quantity for 6 Persons.

1¼ pts. of milk
¼ lb. of sweet chocolate
4 tbsps. of flour
¼ lb. of sugar
¾ cup of butter
7 eggs
1 tsp. of vanilla

Preparation: The chocolate is grated and mixed with flour and sugar. The milk is brought to boil and the chocolate with the flour and sugar added, stirred over the fire until the mixture is thick, then cooled. Cream the butter with the yolks of eggs and vanilla, mix with the chocolate batter and the beaten whites of eggs. Butter a pudding dish, fill in the pudding and bake in oven for 1 hour.

No.39—BAKEDAPPLEANDF ARINAPUDDING.

Quantity for 6 Persons.

1 pt. of milk
½ cup of fine farina
4 eggs
¼ lb. of butter
6 large sweet-sour apples
¼ lb. of raisins or currants
⅛ lb. blanched, ground sweet almonds
6 blanched, ground bitter almonds

One lemon peel

Preparation: The milk is brought to boil, the farina added and cooked 10 minutes, stirring constantly, then cooled. Cream the butter, mix with yolks of eggs, sugar, grated lemon peel, the boiled farina, and the beaten whites of eggs.

The apples are peeled, sliced into ¼ inch slices, mixed with ½ cup of sugar. Butter a pudding dish and put in layers of farina, apples, currants and almonds alternating, repeat 3 times; then bake in oven for 1 hour.

No.40—BAKEDAPPLESTEWPUDDING.

Quantity for 6 Persons.

⅛ lb. of good butter
8 medium-sized sweet-sour apples
½ cup of sugar
1½ heaping tbsps. of flour
1 pt. thick sweet cream
4 eggs
1 lemon peel

Preparation: The apples are peeled, cut into 4 inch slices and stewed in ⅛ lb. of butter, then cooled. Beat 4 yolks of eggs for 30 minutes with sugar, add flour, grated lemon peel, cream and the stewed apples. Lastly add the beaten whites of eggs. Butter a pudding dish, put in the pudding and bake 45 minutes.

No.41—FINEBAKEDAPPLEPUDDING:

Quantity for 6 Persons.

6 medium-sized, sweet-sour apples
½ cup of currants
¼ cup of blanched, ground almonds

2 tbsps. of sugar
¼ tsp. of cinnamon
½ grated lemon peel
¾ qt. thick, sweet cream
5 eggs
½ cup of sugar
2 tbsps. of flour

Preparation: The apples are peeled, cored and filled with a mixture of currants, almonds and 2 tablespoonfuls of sugar. Butter a pudding dish, put in the filled apples, make a batter of cream, cinnamon, lemon peel, yolks of eggs, sugar, flour and beaten whites of eggs, then pour over the apples and bake slowly.

No.42—BAKEDOMELETPUDDING.

Quantity for 6 Persons.

6 eggs
½ grated lemon peel
6 tbsps. of sugar

Preparation: The yolks of eggs are beaten 25 minutes with the sugar, the beaten whites of eggs lightly mixed in, then put into a buttered pudding dish, and bake in oven 20 minutes.

No.43—BAKEDCREAMPUDDING.

Quantity for 6–8 Persons.

1 pt. of milk
7 eggs
⅛ lb. of corn starch
1 tbsp. of butter
½ grated lemon peel

⅛ lb. of sugar

Preparation: Milk, butter and sugar are brought to boil. Four yolks of eggs are stirred smooth with the corn starch and added to the boiling milk to cook 3 minutes, stirring constantly; then cooled and three yolks of eggs, grated lemon peel, beaten whites of 7 eggs added.

Butter a dish, put in the pudding and bake in oven ½ hour. Serve with a fruit sauce.

No.44—BAKEDFLOURPUDDING.

Quantity for 6 Persons.

¾ qt. of milk
½ cup of flour
¼ lb. of sugar
¼ lb. blanched, ground almonds
5 eggs

Preparation: Flour and ½ cup of milk are stirred smooth, the rest of the milk brought to boil and the flour stirred in to boil 1 minute. The almonds, sugar and eggs are stirred in and beaten 10 minutes. Butter a pudding dish, put in the batter and bake in oven for 1 hour. Serve with a raspberry sauce.

No.45—BAKEDSPONGEPUDDING.

Quantity for 6 Persons.

6 eggs
4 tbsps. of thick, sour cream
¾ cup of sugar
2 tsps. of vanilla

Preparation: Yolks of eggs, cream, sugar and vanilla are stirred 20 minutes. The beaten whites of eggs are mixed and put into a buttered pudding dish. Bake in medium hot oven for ½ hour. A fruit sauce is served with it.

No.46—BAKED VEAL ROAST PUDDING.

Quantity for 6–8 Persons.

Ingredients and preparation are given in Chapter 3, Veal, No. 6, Veal Roast Pudding.

No.47—BAKED SWEET PUDDING WITH WINE FROSTING.

Quantity for 6 Persons.

6 rolls
1 pt. of milk
¼ lb. of good butter
¼ lb. of sugar
⅛ lb. chopped citron or almonds
1¼ grated lemon peel
¼ tsp. of cinnamon
6 eggs

For Wine Frosting.

6 eggs
⅛ lb. of sugar
Peel and juice of 1 lemon
¼ tsp. of cinnamon
2 glasses of French white wine
1 glass of arrack

Preparation: The crust is grated off the rolls, these are cut up, soaked in milk for 1 hour, then the milk is pressed out and the soaked rolls stirred with the melted butter to a creamy mass. Add sugar, citron, cinnamon, 6 yolks of eggs, and the beaten whites. Butter a pudding dish, put in the batter and bake 1 hour.

Prepare the frosting by mixing 6 yolks of eggs, sugar, grated lemon peel and lemon juice, cinnamon, French white wine and arrack and heating it on the fire while beating constantly. Then add the 6 beaten whites of eggs to the hot sauce. Pour the wine sauce over the hot baked pudding and serve at once.

No.48—BAKED RYE BREAD PUDDING WITH APPLES.

Quantity for 6 Persons.

2½ cups of soaked rye bread
3 eggs
1 cup of sugar
6–8 medium-sized, sweet-sour apples
⅛ lb. of butter
¾ cup of currants

Preparation: The apples are peeled, cored, cut into slices ¼ inch thick. Cream the butter, add sugar, yolks of eggs, rye bread, currants and beaten whites of eggs. Butter a pudding dish and fill it with alternating layers of rye bread mixture and apples with sugar sprinkled over, repeat 2 or 3 times. The top layer should be rye bread. Put on small pieces of butter and bake in oven 1 hour. Serve sweet cream with the pudding.

No.49—BAKED NOODLE PUDDING.

Quantity for 6 Persons.

Noodles made front 2 eggs
Salt water
6–8 medium-sized, sweet-sour apples
¾ cup of sugar
½ cup of currants
1 cup of water

Preparation: The noodles are cooked in salt water for 10 minutes, then the water is drained off. The apples are peeled, cored and sliced. Butter a pudding dish and fill with alternating layers of noodles and apples with sugar and currants. The top layer should be noodles. Pour on a cup of water, put on small pieces of butter and bake in oven 1 hour.

No.50—BAKEDQUINCEPUDDING.

Quantity for 6 Persons.

6–8 quinces
¼ lb. of sugar
Juice and peel of 1 lemon
6 eggs

Preparation: The quinces are boiled until soft in water, then skin and grate them. The grated quince should weigh about ¾ lb. Stir until white. Add sugar, grated lemon peel and juice, yolks and beaten whites of eggs. Put into a buttered dish and bake in oven ½ hour.

No.51—BAKEDMACAROONPUDDING.

Quantity for 6 Persons.

2 tbsps. of butter
½ pt. of milk
Scant ⅛ lb. of flour
2 tbsps. of cream

3 cups of sweet macaroons
¼ cup of bitter macaroons
5 eggs
⅛ lb. of sugar
⅛ lb. blanched, ground almonds
1 tbsp. of vanilla

Preparation: Butter, milk, flour, crushed macaroons are stirred over the fire until they form a thick batter; remove from the fire and stir until it has cooled off. Add the yolks of eggs, sugar, almonds, vanilla, beaten whites of eggs. Put into a buttered dish and bake in oven for 1 hour. Serve with a fruit sauce.

Remarks: This pudding may be steamed for 1½ hours.

Sweetmeats Baked or Fried in Pans On the Stove.

No.52—FRENCHT OAST.

Quantity for 6 Persons.

6 milk rolls
1 pt. of cream or milk
¼ cup of sugar
2 eggs
½ tsp. of cinnamon
Butter or lard for baking

Preparation: The rolls are sliced, cream, sugar, eggs, cinnamon are mixed and poured over the slices to soak. Butter is heated in a pan, the roll slices baked a golden yellow in it and sprinkled thickly with sugar and cinnamon. Serve dried or fresh fruit sauce with it.

No.53—CAR THUSIANDUMPLINGSWITHWINE SAUCE.

Quantity for 6 Persons.

    6 fresh rolls
    1½ pts. of milk
    2 eggs
    ¼ cup of sugar
    ½ tsp. of cinnamon
    Butter for baking

Preparation: The crust of the rolls is grated off, then quarter them and soak in a pint of milk. After soaking, press out the milk, mix the milk well with eggs, sugar, cinnamon and pour it back on the roll slices to soak for a while longer. Now roll each piece in the crumbs from the crusts and bake in butter to a nice color. Serve on a hot platter with wine sauce.

No.54—APPLEFRITTERSORBANANAFRITTERS.

Quantity for 6 Persons.

    4 sweet-sour apples or bananas
    ½ glass of white wine
    ½ cup of sugar

FortheBatter .

    3 eggs
    ¼ tsp. of salt
    1 cup of flour
    1½ cups of milk
    Butter for frying

Preparation: The apples are peeled, the core removed, sliced in ½ inch thick, round slices, white wine and sugar poured over. Eggs, milk, flour and salt are mixed to a batter. Butter is heated in a pan, each apple slice dipped into the batter, put into the hot butter and fried a nice color. Serve on a hot platter, sprinkled with sugar and cinnamon.

No.55—APPLESTRUDEL.

Quantity for 6 Persons.

Noodle dough from 3 eggs
Flour
⅛ lb. of butter

FortheFilling.

6 medium-sized, sweet-sour apples
½ cup of sugar
½ cup of currants
½ tsp. of cinnamon
¼ lb. blanched, chopped almonds
¼ cup of chopped citron
Butter for baking

Preparation: The noodle dough is rolled out very thin. Melt the butter and brush it on the dough. Peel and core the apples and slice them thin. Then put the apple slices, sugar, cinnamon, almonds and citron on the dough, roll it up, brush it with butter and bake in a buttered pan 30 to 45 minutes. Sprinkle with sugar and cinnamon and serve.

No. 56—CHOCOLATE STRUDEL.

Quantity for 6 Persons.

Noodle dough from 3 eggs
⅛ lb. of butter
Flour

For the Filling.

5 eggs
Scant ½ cup of sugar
⅛ lb. blanched, chopped sweet almonds
10 blanched, chopped bitter almonds
⅓ lb. grated sweet chocolate
Butter for baking

Preparation: The noodle dough is kneaded with ⅛ lb. of butter, then rolled out very thin. The 5 yolks of eggs are stirred with sugar for 15 minutes, almonds and chocolate are added, and lastly the beaten whites of eggs. This mixture is spread on the dough which is then rolled up. A baking pan is buttered and the strudel baked ½ to ¾ hour.

No. 57—CHOCOLATE STRUDEL WITH DRESSING.

Quantity for 6 Persons.

The ingredients and preparation are the same as given under No. 56, Chocolate Strudel. When ready to be baked, place it into the pan in the form of a snail, pour on ¾ pt. of hot cream mixed with ⅛ lb. of fine grated chocolate and 1 tablespoonful of vanilla, then bake ½ hour.

No. 58—STEAM NOODLES.

Quantity for 6 Persons.

⅛ lb. of flour
½ pt. of milk
1 cent's worth of yeast
¼ lb. of butter
3 eggs
1½ cups of flour
1 qt. of cream
⅛ lb. of butter
½ cup of sugar

Preparation: Mix flour, milk and yeast to a batter and set to rise. When risen, mix in butter, sugar, eggs and flour. Put on a well-floured baking board and form dumplings from the dough, leaving them on the board to rise. Stew them 15 minutes in the hot cream and ⅛ lb. of butter until light brown, then sprinkle with sugar and pour drawn butter over.

No. 59—FRIED APPLE POCKETS.

Quantity for 6 Persons.

6 small apples
½ cup of sugar
Raspberry jelly

Pancake Batter.

3 eggs
¾ cup of milk
Salt
2 cups of flour
Lard for baking

Preparation: The apples are pared, cored, filled with jelly and strewn with sugar.

Eggs, milk, salt and flour are stirred into a dough that is rolled out to ¼ inch thickness. With a tumbler cut out 12 round disks. Put each apple between two disks and press the edges together, so as to completely cover the apple. Then fry in much hot lard, place into a colander to drain off the fat and sprinkle with sugar and cinnamon. They may be served warm or cold.

No. 60—BISCUIT TORTONI. MACAROON MOUSSE.

Quantity for 6 Persons.

6 eggs
1 cup of powdered sugar
1 tsp. vanilla
1 cup of grated macaroons
1 pt. whipped cream

Preparation: Whip the yolks of eggs, vanilla and sugar well, mix in the macaroons, beaten whites of eggs and whipped cream. Oil a mold, put in the mixture and let it stand in ice 6 hours before serving.

No. 61—RUM CREAM WITH CHERRY SAUCE.

Quantity for 6–10 Persons.

6 eggs
¾ cup of rum
¼ lb. of sugar
1½ tsps. of vanilla
5 layers of gelatine or ½ package
½ pt. of milk
1 pt. whipped cream

Preparation: Yolks of eggs, rum and sugar are whipped to a froth. Milk and vanilla are brought to boil, the gelatine dissolved in a little milk and mixed with the boiling milk to which also the mixture of yolks of eggs, rum and sugar is added. This mixture must be stirred until it is cold, then the beaten whites of eggs and finally the whipped cream is stirred in. Rinse a mold with cold water, put in the pudding and place on ice or in a cold place. Turn the pudding out on a platter and serve with cherry sauce.

No. 62—WHIPPED CREAM PUDDING.

Quantity for 6 Persons.

1 pt. of whipped cream
½ cup of sugar
2 tsps. of vanilla
2 qts. of fresh strawberries
1 cup of sugar
1 cup of grated pumpernickel
¼ lb. of grated chocolate
¼ cup of sugar

Preparation: The cream is mixed with sugar and vanilla. The strawberries are cleaned and mixed with 1 cup of sugar. Pumpernickel, chocolate and ¼ cup of sugar are mixed. Now arrange in a glass dish layers of strawberries, pumpernickel and whipped cream. The latter garnished with strawberries make the top layer.

No. 63—WINE PUDDING.

Quantity for 6 Persons.

¾ pt. good white wine
Juice of 2 lemons
1 grated lemon rind
½ lb. of sugar
8 eggs
4 layers or ⅓ package of white gelatine

Fruit for garnishing

Preparation: White wine, lemon juice, and lemon rind, sugar, 8 yolks of eggs are stirred well on the stove and brought to boil ¼ minute. The gelatine is dissolved in 4 tablespoonfuls of wine and mixed in with the rest, also the beaten whites of eggs. Oil a mold, put in the mixture and put on ice or in a cold place. When stiff, turn it out on a platter and garnish with fruit.

No. 64—WINE CREAM.

Quantity for 6 Persons.

¾ pt. good white wine
¼ cup of French brandy or cognac
½ cup of cherry juice
Juice of 1 lemon
¼ lb. of sugar
6 eggs
6 layers or ½ package of red gelatine
Juice of 1 orange
1 pinch of salt

Preparation: White wine, brandy, cherry juice, lemon juice, orange juice, sugar, yolks of eggs and the gelatine dissolved in wine are mixed well and stirred over a slow fire until it thickens, but do not let it boil. While still warm, add the whites of eggs beaten to a froth and salt. Oil a mold, put in the cream and place on ice or prepare it a day before using. When serving, turn it out and garnish with cherries.

No. 65—WINE JELLY WITH RICE LAYERS.

Quantity for 6 Persons.

Wine Jelly.

½ bottle of white wine

9 layers of gelatine or ¾ package
1½ cups of water
Juice of 2 lemons and 1 orange

Rice Layer.

¼ lb. of sugar
¾ cup of good rice
3 qts. of water
Juice and grated rind of ½ lemon
1 pinch of salt
½ pt. of white wine
3 layers or ¼ package of white gelatine
3 oranges

Preparation: White wine, lemon and orange juice, sugar and gelatine dissolved in 1½ cups of water are well mixed over a slow fire. The rice is washed and cooked 25 minutes in 3 qts. of water, then poured into a colander or sieve. Now add the wine, sugar, lemon juice and rind, salt and dissolved gelatine, cover and cook very slowly. When the juice has been absorbed by the rice, take it from the stove and cool. A dish is placed into ice or very cold water and a layer of wine jelly poured in to stiffen. When that is stiff, cut out oblong dumplings of cold rice and place them on the jelly layer in circles, pour on another layer of wine jelly and so on until the rice and jelly are used up. When stiff, turn it out and garnish the jelly and platter with orange slices.

No. 66—WHITE WINE JELLY WITH FRUIT LAYERS.

Quantity for 6 Persons.

½ bottle of white wine
9 layers or ¾ package of white gelatine
¾ pt. of water
¾ cup of sugar
Juice of 2 lemons and one orange

Fruit for Layers.

Bananas
Strawberries or pineapples

Preparation: White wine, dissolved gelatine, sugar, lemon and orange juice are well mixed and stirred over the fire until it starts to boil, then strain through a cloth. Place a dish on ice or into very cold water, pour in a cup of jelly to stiffen, on this place a layer of fruit, strawberries, sliced bananas or pineapples and repeat several times.

If you have no fresh fruit, use preserves from which the syrup has been drained. The jelly layer must be on top. Turn it out before serving. The platter may be garnished with various kinds of fruit.

No. 67—LEMON JELLY.

Quantity for 6 Persons.

¾ qt. of water
Juice of 4 to 5 lemons
10 layers or 1 package of white gelatine
½ lb. of sugar

Preparation: The gelatine is dissolved in ¾ qt. of warm water, sugar and lemon juice added and the whole warmed a little, then strained through a cloth. Put into a mold and when stiff, turn it out on a platter.

Remarks: You may put layers of fruit into the jelly according to No. 66, Wine Jelly With Fruit Layers.

No. 68—ORANGE JELLY.

Quantity for 6 Persons.

1¼ pts. of orange juice, (about 10 oranges)

5 tbsps. of lemon juice
¼ lb. of sugar
9 layers or ¾ package of red gelatine
1 cup of champagne or good white wine

Preparation: The oranges are cleaned, cut into halves, and the juice carefully pressed out with a lemon squeezer. The gelatine and sugar are dissolved in this juice, then warmed and lemon juice and wine added. Strain through a cloth. The orange rinds are carefully cleaned out without breaking them and filled with the above gelatine, then placed on ice. When stiff, place the oranges on a platter and garnish with fresh leaves.

No. 69—PINEAPPLE JELLY.

Quantity for 6 Persons.

1 large pineapple
1 pt. of water or white wine
8 layers or ¾ package of white gelatine
1½ cups of sugar

Preparation: The pineapple is peeled and grated on a fine grater. The gelatine is dissolved in 1 pt. of warm water, then mixed well with sugar and the grated pineapple. This mixture is strained through a fine sieve, poured into a mold, placed on ice to harden. When cold, turn it out.

No. 70—CHERRY JELLY.

Quantity for 6 Persons.

2 qts. of sour cherries
1 pt. of water
½ lb. of sugar
1 stick of cinnamon
10 layers or 1 package of gelatine

½ cup of red wine
2 cloves

Preparation: The cherries are cleaned and stoned. Two dozen of the stones are crushed and boiled with the crushed cherries, cloves and cinnamon for 20 minutes in 1 pt. of water, the dish being covered. Strain, add gelatine and sugar, then strain again and add the red wine. Put the jelly into a mold, place on ice and when cold, turn out on a platter.

No. 71—STRAWBERRY JELLY.

Quantity for 6 Persons.

2 qts. of nice, ripe strawberries
¾ lb. of sugar
Juice of 2 lemons
8 layers or ¾ package of red gelatine
2 tsps. of vanilla
1 pt. of water

Preparation: The strawberries are crushed, water, sugar, lemon juice mixed in and cooked over a slow fire for 10 minutes, then strained through a fine sieve. The gelatine is dissolved in this juice and the whole strained again. Fill into a mold, place on ice to stiffen, then turn out and garnish with strawberries and whipped cream.

No. 72—ORANGE GELATINE.

Quantity for 6 Persons.

1 pt. of cream
Grated rind of 1 orange
Juice of 3 oranges
6 layers or ½ package of white gelatine
½ lb. of sugar

Preparation: Cream, grated orange rind and juice, sugar and gelatine are mixed well and cooked ¼ hour, stirring constantly, then strained through a fine sieve. Oil a mold, put in the jelly and place on ice or prepare the day before serving. Turn out on a platter or glass dish.

No. 73—ARRACK CREAM WITH WHIPPED CREAM.

Quantity for 6 Persons.

6 yolks of eggs
½ lb. of sugar
5 layers or ½ package of red gelatine
½ cup of warm water
6 tbsps. of arrack
1 pt. of whipped cream

Preparation: Yolks of eggs and sugar are whipped ½ hour. The gelatine is dissolved in warm water and strained, then mixed with the yolks of eggs and sugar, arrack and lastly the whipped cream. This is filled into a glass dish and set to stiffen.

No. 74—STRAWBERRY CREAM.

Quantity for 6 Persons.

1 qt. of preserved strawberries, or 2 qts. of fresh ones
¼ lb. of sugar
1 tsp. of vanilla
5 layers or ½ package of white gelatine
½ cup of warm juice
1 pt. of whipped cream
12 lady fingers

Preparation: The juice is drained from the strawberries and strained to remove the seeds. The gelatine is dissolved in ½ cup of the juice and mixed with strawberries, vanilla, sugar and whipped cream. Oil a mold, strew with sugar, put in a layer of lady fingers, then the cream on top of the lady fingers, place on ice to harden, turn it out and serve with strawberry juice.

Remarks: If you take fresh strawberries, use more sugar.

No. 75—RASPBERRY CREAM.

Quantity for 6 Persons.

Ingredients and preparation are the same as given under No. 74, Strawberry Cream. If you use fresh raspberries, you need 2 pts.

No. 76—PINEAPPLE CREAM.

Quantity for 6 Persons.

1 pt. of preserved pineapple
½ cup of sugar
1 tsp. of vanilla
6 layers or ½ package of white gelatine
1 pt. whipped cream

Preparation: The juice from the pineapple is drained off and warmed, the gelatine dissolved in some of it and strained through a fine sieve. Sugar and vanilla are stirred in and the pineapple cut up into small pieces. Lastly add the whipped cream which has been drained on a sieve. Oil a mold, strew in a little sugar, fill in the cream and place on ice or prepare the day before serving. Turn out on a platter.

No. 77—VANILLA CREAM.

Quantity for 6 Persons.

½ pt. of milk

3 eggs
1 vanilla bean or 2 tbsps. of vanilla
5 layers or ½ package of gelatine
1 pt. of whipped cream
¼ lb. of sugar

Preparation: The vanilla bean is put into the milk to soak, or the vanilla extract put into the milk; also the yolks of eggs, sugar and gelatine. Let this mixture come to a boil, stirring constantly, boil ¼ minute, mix in the beaten whites of eggs and stir until cold. Now add the whipped cream. Oil a mold, fill in the cream, and place on ice; turn it out when stiff.

No. 78—COLD APPLE CREAM.

Quantity for 6 Persons.

6 apples
½ pt. white wine
½ lb. of sugar
1 qt. of cream
5 eggs
1 tbsp. of flour
½ lemon peel
1 qt. of strawberries or raspberries

Preparation: The apples are peeled, cored and cut into 8 parts, then boiled until soft in ½ pt. of white wine and ¼ lb. of sugar. When done, cool them.

The cream, yolks of eggs, flour, grated lemon peel and ¼ lb. of sugar are mixed well, then boiled to a cream, stirring constantly. Now oil a mold and put in a layer of boiled apples, then strawberries or raspberries, then a layer of cream, then frosting made of the whites of eggs beaten to a froth with 6 tablespoonfuls of sugar. This is baked 10 minutes in a medium hot oven. Let it get cold and serve in the dish.

Remarks. This cream may be served hot, but it is better cold. If you have no fresh fruit, use preserved, but drain off the juice.

No. 79—COLD APPLE PUDDING.

Quantity for 6 Persons.

12 sweet-sour apples
Water
2 cups of white wine
8 layers or ½ package of white gelatine
1 cup of sugar

Preparation: The apples are cut up and put into a pot with enough water to cover them, then boiled until soft, very slowly, so they do not get slushy. Pour them into a sieve or cloth and drain off the juice. This is boiled down to 1 qt., add to it the sugar and gelatine and strain; boil up again, then mix in the white wine. Fill the whole into a glass dish to stiffen and serve with a vanilla sauce.

Remarks: The apples may be used for apple sauce.

No. 80—NECTAR.

Quantity for 6 Persons.

1 qt. of sour cream
½ lb. of sugar
1½ tsps. of vanilla
9 layers or ¾ package of red gelatine
4 tbsps. of rum
¼ cup of milk

Preparation:

Sour cream, sugar, vanilla and rum are mixed well. The gelatine is dissolved in warm milk, strained and mixed with the other ingredients. Pour into a mold and set on ice to stiffen. Turn it out before serving.

No. 81—CORN STARCH PUDDING.

Quantity for 6–8 Persons.

1 qt. of milk
Scant ¼ lb. of corn starch
¼ lb. of sugar
⅛ lb. peeled, ground almonds
1 tbsp. of vanilla
8 eggs

Preparation: ¾ qt. of milk, sugar, almonds and vanilla are mixed well and brought to boil. Then the corn starch is stirred into ¼ qt. of milk, poured into the boiling mixture and boiled 5 minutes, stirring constantly. Yolks of eggs are stirred in as soon as the pudding is taken from the fire, also the beaten whites of eggs. Put into a dish to stiffen, turn it out and serve with a vanilla or wine sauce.

No. 82—COLD LEMON CREAM.

Quantity for 6 Persons.

6 eggs
½ lb. of sugar
Juice and rind of 1 lemon
½ glass white wine
5 layers or ½ package of white gelatine
3 tbsps. of arrack

Preparation: The yolks of eggs and sugar are stirred 1 hour, then add the grated rind and juice of 1 lemon and the arrack. Dissolve the gelatine in warm white wine, stir until cold and strain before mixing with the other ingredients. Add the whites of eggs beaten to a froth, place on ice or prepare a day before serving. Turn it out on a platter.

No. 83—RUSSIAN CREAM.

Quantity for 6 Persons.

6 eggs
¾ cup of sugar
2 tbsps. of rum

Preparation: Yolks of eggs and sugar are beaten for 15 minutes, add the rum, then the beaten whites of eggs. Serve in glass dishes.

No. 84—ORANGE CREAM PREPARED COLD.

Quantity for 6 Persons.

5 eggs
½ lb. of sugar
Grated rind of ½ orange
2 tbsps. lemon juice
4 layers or ⅓ package of white gelatine
8 tbsps. of orange juice

Preparation: The yolks of eggs and sugar are beaten ½ hour, add the gelatine dissolved in the orange juice, and strained. Then add the lemon juice, grated orange rind and the beaten whites of eggs. Put into glass dishes and set to stiffen.

No. 85—COLD LEMON CREAM.

Quantity for 6 Persons.

The preparation is the same as given under No. 84, Orange Cream Prepared Cold. Instead of 8 tablespoonfuls of orange juice and rind, take the same quantity of lemon juice and rind.

No. 86—COFFEE CREAM PREPARED COLD.

Quantity for 6 Persons.

The preparation is the same as given under No. 84, Orange Cream Prepared Cold. Instead of the juice of oranges, the juice of lemons and the rind, take ¼ pt. of coffee extract in which you dissolve 1 tablespoonful of cocoa.

No. 87—CHOCOLATE CREAM PREPARED COLD.

Quantity for 6 Persons.

The preparation is the same as given under No. 84, Orange Cream Prepared Cold. Instead of the juice of oranges, the juice of lemons and the rind, take 1/10 lb. of bitter chocolate or cocoa dissolved in ¼ cup of water and 1 teaspoonful of vanilla.

No. 88—CHOCOLATE CREAM.

Quantity for 6 Persons.

¼ lb. of chocolate
⅛ lb. of sugar
1 pt. of water
6 layers or scant ½ package of white gelatine
4 eggs
1 tsp. of vanilla

Preparation: The chocolate is dissolved in ½ pt. of water and the gelatine in the other ½ pt., mix the two. Add sugar and vanilla and boil this mixture ½ minute. Take from the fire and add the yolks of eggs, a little later the whites of eggs beaten to a froth. Rinse a mold with cold water, put in the mixture to stiffen, turn it out and serve with a vanilla sauce.

No. 89—CHOCOLATE MOUSSE.

Quantity for 6 Persons.

½ cup of cocoa
¾ cup of sugar
1 tbsp. vanilla
4 layers or ⅓ package of gelatine
½ cup of water
1 pt. of whipped cream

Preparation: Dissolve the cocoa and gelatine in ½ cup of water on a small fire, with sugar and vanilla well mixed in. Stir until cold, add the whipped cream. Rinse a mold with cold water; put in the mixture, close the dish well, pack in ice and salt and let stand several hours. When serving, dry the dish and turn the cream out on a platter.

No. 90—VANILLA MOUSSE.

Quantity for 6 Persons.

1 qt. of whipped cream
4 layers or ⅓ package of white gelatine
5 tbsps. of warm water
2 tsps. of good vanilla
½ lb. of sugar

Preparation.: The gelatine is dissolved in the warm water and strained. The sugar and vanilla are added and the whipped cream in spoonfuls. Rinse a mold with cold water, fill in the mixture, close well and pack in ice and salt for several hours. Then dry and turn out on a platter.

No. 91—COFFEE MOUSSE.

Quantity for 6 Persons.

The preparation is the same as given under No. 90, Vanilla Mousse. Instead of vanilla, take 6 to 8 tablespoonfuls of coffee extract.

No. 92—HAZELNUT MOUSSE.

Quantity for 6 Persons.

The preparation is the same as given under No. 90, Vanilla Mousse. Mix in ¼ lb. roasted, coarsely chopped hazelnuts.

No. 93—PINEAPPLE MOUSSE.

Quantity for 6 Persons.

The preparation is the same as given under No. 90. Instead of vanilla, take ½ lb. of pineapple, cut into small pieces, or pineapple puree.

No. 94—RUM OR COGNAC MOUSSE.

Quantity for 6 Persons.

The preparation is the same as given under No. 90, Vanilla Mousse. Instead of vanilla, take 8 tablespoonfuls of rum or cognac.

No. 95—COUNT PUECKLER OR LAYER MOUSSE.

Quantity for 6 Persons.

1½ pts. whipped cream
½ lb. chocolate
½ lb. of sugar

½ cup of raspberry jelly
2 whites of eggs
⅛ lb. of macaroons
1½ tsps. of vanilla
12 layers or 1 package of white gelatine
½ cup of warm water

PART I.

Preparation: ½ lb. of chocolate is grated and mixed well with ¼ cup of warm water and ⅛ lb. of sugar. Dissolve the gelatine in the other ¼ cup of warm water, strain and divide into 3 parts; mix ⅓ of it with the chocolate, ½ teaspoonful of vanilla and ½ pt. of thick whipped cream.

PART II.

Dissolve the raspberry jelly over the fire, mix in ⅛ lb. of sugar, 2 beaten whites of eggs, and ⅓ of the dissolved gelatine, also ½ teaspoonful of vanilla and ½ pt. of thick whipped cream.

PART III.

The macaroons are crushed, mixed with ½ pt. of whipped cream, ⅛ lb. of sugar, ½ teaspoonful of vanilla and ⅓ part of the dissolved gelatine.

A form is rinsed with cold water and layers of the chocolate, raspberry and macaroon mixtures are put in. Then the mold is closed well and packed in salt and ice for some hours. When serving, dry the mold and turn it out on a platter.

No. 96—COLD RICE STARCH PUDDING.

Quantity for 6 Persons.

¼ lb. rice starch
¼ lb. of sugar
1 pt. of milk
1 grated lemon peel
5 eggs

1 pinch of salt

Preparation: The milk and grated lemon peel are brought to boil; sugar, rice starch and yolks of eggs are mixed well with a little cold milk, stirred into the boiling milk and boiled again 5 minutes, stirring constantly; then take from the stove. When the mass has cooled, mix in the beaten whites of eggs. Rinse a mold with cold water, fill in the pudding and set to stiffen. Turn it out on a platter and serve with a fruit sauce.

No. 97—COLD CHOCOLATE PUDDING WITH FARINA.

Quantity for 6 Persons.

½ lb. of fine chocolate
⅛ lb. of fine farina
½ cup of sugar
1 qt. of milk
1 tsp. of vanilla

Preparation: The chocolate is grated and mixed with farina, vanilla and sugar. The milk is brought to boil, the farina mixture put in and boiled 15 minutes, stirring constantly. Rinse a mold with cold water, fill in the pudding and set to stiffen. Vanilla sauce is served with it.

No. 98—COLD RICE PUDDING WITH PEACHES.

Quantity for 6–10 Persons.

1 cup of good rice
¾ qt. of milk
1 pinch of salt
1 cup of sugar
1 tsp. of vanilla
½ cup of raisins

1 cup of blanched, ground almonds
5 finely chopped macaroons
5 layers or ½ package of white gelatine
1 pt. of whipped cream
1 qt. preserved or fresh stewed peaches

Preparation: Wash and boil the rice for 5 minutes in 1 cup of water with a pinch of salt, then add the milk gradually and cook until the rice is done and thick, but not mushy. Mix with sugar, vanilla, raisins, almonds and macaroons. Dissolve the gelatine in ¼ cup of warm water and mix with the rice, then cool and stir in the whipped cream. Rinse a mold with milk and sprinkle with sugar, then make alternating layers of rice and peaches from which the syrup has been drained. The top layer must be rice. Close the mold well and place on ice or into a very cold place. When serving, use the fruit juice for a sauce.

No. 99—PLAIN COLD RICE PUDDING.

Quantity for 6 Persons.

1 cup of rice
¾ qt. of milk
1 cup of sugar
1 tsp. of vanilla
5 layers or ½ package of white gelatine
1 pt. of whipped cream
1 pinch of salt

Preparation: Wash and boil the rice 5 minutes in 1 cup of water and a pinch of salt, then gradually add the milk until the rice is thick, but not mushy. Now stir in the sugar and vanilla. Dissolve the gelatine in ¼ cup of warm water and stir into the rice, then cool and mix in the whipped cream. Rinse a mold or dish with milk and sprinkle with sugar. Put in the pudding, close it well and place on ice or into very cold water. Turn it out on a platter and serve with cherry sauce.

No. 100—CHAMPAGNE CREAM.

Quantity for 6 Persons.

8 eggs
Scant ½ lb. of sugar
1 pt. champagne
5 layers or ½ package of white gelatine
1 pint of thick whipped cream

Preparation: 5 yolks of eggs, 3 whole eggs, sugar and champagne are mixed and boiled to cream, stirring constantly. The gelatine is dissolved in ¼ cup of water and mixed into the cream, also the beaten whites of 5 eggs. Put it into a mold or into glasses and put on ice. Serve with macaroons.

Remarks: Omit the gelatine when using the whipped cream.

No. 101—CURRANT AND RASPBERRY PUDDING.

Quantity for 6 Persons.

2 qts. of currants and 1 qt. raspberries
1 pt. of water
¾ lb. of sugar
1 cup of fine farina or sago
¾ cup of corn starch

Preparation: Currants and raspberries are picked over and cooked in 1 pt. of water ½ hour, then strained through a cloth and the juice brought to boil. Add the sugar and farina and cook for 20 minutes, stirring constantly; fill the mass into a mold rinsed with cold water to stiffen. Turn it out and serve with cream or milk.

Remarks: If you use corn starch instead of farina, mix it with 1 cup of cold juice before putting it into the boiling juice. Then boil it 5 to 8 minutes and fill it into the mold. If the farina is not sweet enough, add more sugar while boiling.

No. 102—GOOSEBERRY PUDDING.

Quantity for 6 Persons.

2 qts. of gooseberries
1 qt. of water
1 lb. of sugar
¾ cup of fine farina

Preparation: Gooseberries are best when still unripe. Cook them in water for ½ hour, then press through a fine sieve and put in the sugar and cook again with the farina for 10 minutes. Fill it into a dish rinsed with cold water and set aside to stiffen, turn it out and serve with cream or milk.

No. 103—CHERRY PUDDING.

Quantity for 6 Persons.

2 lbs. of sour cherries
1 pt. of water
¼ lb. of sugar
1 tbsp. of lemon juice
¼ lb. of corn starch

Preparation: Clean and stone the cherries, then crush about 20 stones and cook them with the cherries in the water slowly for ½ hour, after that strain them and add lemon juice and sugar. Then let it come to boil again. Mix the corn starch with 1 cup of cold juice and stir it into the boiling juice to cook 5 to 8 minutes more, stirring constantly. Put into a dish rinsed with cold water and after stiffening, turn it out and serve with cream or milk.

Remarks: If the pudding is too thin, add more corn starch.

No. 104—HILL CREAM.

Quantity for 6 Persons.

¾ qt. sweet cream
5 yolks of eggs
½ lemon peel
1 tbsp. of flour
¼ lb. of sugar
3 whites of eggs
1 glass of raspberry jelly

Preparation: Cream, yolks of eggs, grated lemon peel, flour and sugar are mixed well and boiled to a cream. The 3 beaten whites of eggs and the jelly are stirred 1 hour, then fill the cream into a glass dish and set to cool. After cooling, fill the jelly on top of it. Serve cold.

Desserts That Are Frozen.

No. 105—VANILLA ICE CREAM.

Quantity for 10 Persons.

1 qt. of cream
1 pt. of milk
¾ tbsp. of flour
2 tbsps. of vanilla
Sugar to taste
3 eggs

Preparation: ½ pt. of milk 3 yolks of eggs and flour are boiled to a cream, stirring constantly; mix the beaten whites of eggs with sugar and add to the cream. To this add the rest of the milk, cream and vanilla. Freeze the mass and pour a hot chocolate sauce over it when serving. It is very fine.

No. 106—STRAWBERRY ICE CREAM.

Quantity for 6 Persons.

3 qts. of fresh or 1 qt. preserved strawberries
1 qt. of cream
1 tsp. of vanilla
Sugar to taste

Preparation,: The strawberries, fresh or preserved, are rubbed through a sieve, cream and vanilla, sugar to taste added, then frozen.

No. 107—RASPBERRY ICE CREAM.

Quantity for 6 Persons.

2 pts. of fresh or 1 pt. preserved raspberries
1 pt. of cream
1 tsp. of vanilla
Sugar to taste

The preparation is the same as given under No. 106, Strawberry Ice Cream.

No. 108—PEACH ICE CREAM.

Quantity for 8–10 Persons.

2½ qts. of fresh or 1 qt. preserved peaches
1 qt. of cream
1 tsp. vanilla
Sugar to taste

Preparation: Fresh peaches are peeled, stoned and rubbed through a sieve, mixed with cream, vanilla and sugar and frozen.

No. 109—APRICOT ICE CREAM.

Quantity for 8–10 Persons.

2½ qts. of fresh or 1 qt. of preserved apricots
1 qt. of cream
1 tsp. of vanilla
Sugar to taste

The preparation is the same as given under No. 108, Peach Ice Cream.

No. 110—LEMON ICE CREAM.

Quantity for 6 Persons.

1 pt. of milk
½ pt. of cream
2 cups of sugar
Juice of 2½ lemons

Preparation: Milk, cream and sugar are mixed and put into the ice cream freezer to freeze a little, then the juice of lemons are added and frozen.

No. 111—PINEAPPLE ICE CREAM.

Quantity for 6–8 Persons.

1 large pineapple
1 qt. of cream
Sugar
Juice of ½ lemon

Preparation: The pineapple is peeled and grated, then rubbed through a sieve, mixed with cream, sugar and lemon juice and frozen.

No. 112—CHOCOLATE ICE CREAM.

Quantity for 6 Persons.

1 pt. of cream
1 pt. of milk
4 yolks of eggs
½ lb. of chocolate
1½ tsps. of vanilla
About ½ lb. of sugar

Preparation: Dissolve the chocolate in milk, add sugar, cream, vanilla, yolks of eggs and heat to the boiling point, stirring constantly. Remove from the fire immediately, stir until cold and freeze.

No. 113—COFFEE ICE CREAM.

Quantity for 6 Persons.

1 pt. of cream
¼ lb. of finely ground strong coffee
1 pt. of milk
½ lb. of sugar
4 yolks of eggs

Preparation: The coffee must steep in the milk for 1 hour, then strain through a fine cloth. Cream, yolks of eggs and sugar are mixed well and cooked to a cream, stirring constantly. Then take it off the stove and stir until cold, mix with coffee and milk and freeze.

No. 114—NUT ICE CREAM.

Quantity for 6 Persons.

1 pt. of cream
1 pt. of milk
About ¼ lb. of sugar
3 yolks of eggs
½ lb. ground hazelnuts

Preparation: Milk, cream, sugar and yolks of eggs are mixed well and boiled, stirring constantly; then cooled, the nuts mixed in and the mass frozen.

Remarks: One teaspoonful of vanilla may be added.

No. 115—TEA ICE CREAM.

Quantity for 6 Persons.

1 pt. of cream
1 pt. of milk
⅛ lb. of sugar
4 yolks of eggs
2 tbsps. of fine tea

The preparation is the same as given under No. 113, Coffee Ice Cream. Instead of steeping the coffee in the milk, put in tea.

No. 116—VANILLA ICE CREAM WITH FRUIT.

Quantity for 6 Persons.

1 qt. of cream

1½ tbsps. of vanilla
¼ lb. of sugar
4 eggs
1 cup of large raisins
¼ cup of chopped citron
¼ lb. of crushed macaroons
25 preserved cherries
3 tbsps. of maraschino

Preparation: Cream, vanilla, sugar and yolks of eggs are mixed well and brought to boil, stirring constantly, then cook it. The raisins are scalded, put into a colander, cut into small pieces, mixed with the cut citron, crushed macaroons and quartered cherries, also 3 tablespoonfuls of maraschino are mixed into the cold cream. Add also the beaten whites of eggs and freeze.

No. 117—STRAWBERRY ICE.

Quantity for 6 Persons.

4 qts. of fresh or 1 qt. preserved strawberries
1 tsp. of vanilla
Sugar to taste

Preparation: The strawberries are rubbed through a sieve, sugar and vanilla added, then frozen. Serve with whipped cream.

No. 118—RASPBERRY ICE.

Quantity for 6 Persons.

3 pts. of fresh or 1 qt. of preserved raspberries
1 tsp. of vanilla
Sugar to taste

The preparation is the same as given under No. 117, Strawberry Ice.

No. 119—PEACH ICE.

Quantity for 6 Persons.

3–4 qts. of fresh or 1½ qts. of preserved peaches
Sugar to taste

Preparation: The fresh peaches are peeled, stoned, pressed through a sieve, mixed with sugar and frozen.

No. 120—APRICOT ICE.

Quantity for 6 Persons.

Preparation and ingredients are the same as given under No. 119, Peach Ice.

No. 121—PINEAPPLE ICE.

Quantity for 6 Persons.

1 large pineapple
½ pt. of water
½ lb. of sugar, (good measure)
2 whites of eggs
Juice of ½ lemon

Preparation: The pineapple is peeled, grated, mixed with sugar, whites of eggs, lemon juice and water, then frozen.

No. 122—TUTTI-FRUTTI ICE.

Quantity for 6 Persons.

1 large pineapple

½ pt. of water
3 whites of eggs
½ lb. of sugar, (good measure)
Juice of ½ lemon
2 oranges
1 cupful of preserved cherries

Preparation: This tutti-frutti ice is prepared like No. 121, Pineapple Ice. Oranges are peeled and cut into small pieces and sugared, the cherries are quartered and sugared. When the pineapple ice is nearly frozen, mix with orange and cherry and freeze a little more, but do not turn the freezer.

No. 123—CHAMPAGNE SHERBET.

Quantity for 6 Persons.

1 pt. of water
1 qt. of champagne
2 cups or 1 pt. of sugar
1 pt. of orange juice

Preparation: Dissolve the sugar in a little water then add champagne and orange juice. Fill the mixture into a freezer and pack with finely chopped ice and salt. Do not turn freezer, stir contents occasionally with spoon.

No. 124—CHAMPAGNE FRAPPE.

Quantity for 8 Persons.

1 pt. of water
Whites of 2 eggs
Juice of 1½ lemons or to taste
2 cups of sugar
1 bottle of champagne

Preparation: Dissolve the sugar in water and add the juice of lemon, beat the whites of eggs well and add, then let it freeze. Before serving the lemon ice, it should be put into a larger dish when taken out of the freezer. Pour the champagne over the mass and beat quickly, serve at once in glasses.

No. 125—MAPLE SYRUP ICE.

Quantity for 8 Persons.

Yolks of 8 eggs
2 tbsps. of water
1 cup of maple syrup
1 qt. of whipped cream

Preparation: The yolks of eggs and water are beaten 15 minutes, add the syrup, let it come to a boil in a double boiler, stirring constantly. Let it cool, add the whipped cream, pour into a mold, close the mold and pack in ice with salt.

No. 126—ROLL DUMPLINGS.

Quantity for 6 Persons.

6 rolls
1 piece of butter, (egg size)
2–3 eggs
½ cup of sugar
1 pinch of salt
1 cup of flour
4 qts. of water mixed with 1 tbsp. of salt

Preparation: The rolls must be soaked in water or milk and the liquid pressed out. Cream the butter with the eggs and sugar, then mix all this with the soaked rolls, flour and salt. Now boil 4 qts. of water with one tablespoonful of salt, cut off dumplings from the batter with a tablespoon, drop into the boiling salt water and boil them 10 minutes. Always try one dumpling first, if too loose, mix a little more flour into the batter.

No. 127—BETTER KIND OF ROLL DUMPLINGS.

Quantity for 6 Persons.

6 rolls
3 eggs
¼ lb. of butter
½ cup of sugar
A pinch of salt
½ cup of currants
¼ lb. of blanched, ground almonds
Rind of ½ lemon
¾ cup of flour
4 qts. of salt water

Preparation: The rolls must be soaked in milk and the milk pressed out. Cream the butter with the yolks of eggs and sugar, add the almonds, currants, grated lemon rind, rolls, flour and salt. Beat the whites of eggs to a stiff froth and stir into the mixture. Let the 4 qts. of salt water boil, cut off dumplings from the batter with a tablespoon, drop into the boiling salt water and boil them 10 minutes.

Remarks: Always try one dumpling first, if too loose, mix a little more flour into the batter.

No. 128—LEMON ICE GARNISHED WITH FRUIT.

Quantity for 6 Persons.

1 pt. of milk
Juice of 1 lemon
1½ cupfuls of sugar

6 slices of canned pineapple
6 boiled prunes
6 tsps. of whipped cream
6 tsps. of brandied cherries
½ cupful of fruit juice
6 preserved apricots cut in half

Preparation: Mix the milk, lemon juice and sugar, but do not freeze. On each dessert plate put a slice of pineapple, on this the half of an apricot, a prune on the apricot, then a teaspoonful of whipped cream, finishing with the brandied cherries, adding a small piece of lemon ice to the fruit. Mix some of the pineapple and apricot juice, boil with sugar and 2 tablespoonfuls of sherry until it thickens. Add 3 tablespoonfuls of this sauce to each plate of dessert.

BEVERAGES.

Cold and Hot Beverages.

No. 1—COLD PUNCH.

2 bottles of white wine
½ bottle of arrack
Juice of 3 lemons
1 lb. of sugar
1 thin lemon rind

Preparation: The ingredients are mixed well, put into a punch bowl and covered to stand several hours.

No. 2—HOT PUNCH.

1 bottle of fine rum
1 bottle of white wine
1½ lbs. sugar
Juice of 2 lemons
Rind of 1 lemon
2½ qts. of boiling water

Preparation: The punch bowl is put into hot water. Pour into it 1 pt. of boiling water, sugar and lemon rind and let stand for a while, then add white wine, rum, lemon juice and 2 qts. of hot water, stir with a wooden ladle and serve hot.

No. 3—HOT KING'S PUNCH.

1 bottle of white wine
1 pt. fine rum
Juice of 1 lemon
½ lemon peel
¾ lb. of sugar
1 qt. of water

Preparation: Mix the ingredients, boil and serve hot.

No. 4—PRESIDENT'S PUNCH.

Cold or Warm.

1 bottle of fine white wine
1 wineglassful of fine rum
3 pts. of water
½ lb. of sugar
⅛ lb. of preserved pineapple
1 cup of pineapple juice

Preparation: Sugar and water are boiled 15 minutes, then wine, rum, pineapple juice and preserved pineapple added. This punch is served hot or put on ice and served cold.

No. 5—EGG PUNCH.

1 bottle of white wine
¾ pt. of arrack
1¼ cups of sugar
½ lemon rind
Juice of 1½ lemon
7 eggs

Preparation: Mix white wine, sugar, lemon juice and rind, add the well beaten eggs and bring to a boil, beating constantly, then take from the stove and mix in the arrack. Serve at once.

No. 6—WARM BURGUNDY PUNCH.

½ bottle of Burgundy wine
½ bottle of good white wine
½ bottle of arrack
½ pt. pineapple juice
2 oranges
½ bottle German champagne
¼ lb. of sugar
¼ pt. of water

Preparation: Sugar, water, Burgundy wine, white wine, arrack and pineapple juice are mixed well and heated but not boiled. The orange is sliced with the peel and put into the bowl, then the hot fluid is poured in and the champagne added at the table.

No. 7—HOT WINE.

1 bottle of red wine
¼ lb. of sugar
10 cloves
1 stick of cinnamon
½ lemon rind

Preparation: The ingredients are mixed well and brought to the boiling point, but not boiled, strained and served hot.

No. 8—GROG.

½ pt. of rum
Liberal ½ lb. of sugar
¾ qt. of boiling water

Preparation: Mix the ingredients and serve at once.

No. 9—BISHOP.

1 tbsp. of Bishop essence, or the thin peel of a small orange
1 bottle of red wine
¼ lb. of sugar
½ cup of water

Preparation: The sugar is dissolved in the red wine and the Bishop essence mixed in or the orange peel is soaked in water for ½ hour and mixed with the wine.

No. 10—CARDINAL, (COLD).

2 bottles of good white wine
Juice of 2 oranges
½ lb. of fresh pineapple
1 bottle of champagne
1 lb. of sugar
½ orange peel

Preparation: The pineapple is cut into small pieces, put into a bowl, the piece of orange peel and juice, with the sugar added and left to stand 15 minutes, then the white wine is poured on. Put the beverage on ice and when serving, add the champagne.

No. 11—CREAM PUNCH.

5 eggs
½ lb. of sugar
1½ qts. of whipped cream
½ pt. of arrack

Preparation: Yolks of eggs and sugar are beaten to a froth, the arrack mixed in, the beaten whites of eggs added and lastly whipped cream. Serve this punch in glasses or tumblers.

No. 12—PINEAPPLE PUNCH.

1 large, fresh pineapple
½ lb. of sugar
2 bottles of white wine
¾ bottle of champagne

Preparation: The pineapple is peeled and sliced very thin. The sugar is added, ½ bottle of the wine poured over and let stand several hours, then add the rest of the wine and when serving, pour in the champagne.

Remarks: Instead of the champagne you may put in a small bottle of Seltzer-water.

No. 13—STRAWBERRY PUNCH.

2 qts. of fresh strawberries
Scant ½ lb. of sugar
2 bottles of white wine

The preparation is the same as No. 12, Pineapple Punch. If you like you may add ½ bottle of champagne.

No. 14—RASPBERRY WINE.

Raspberries and sugar
Light white wine

Preparation: The berries are crushed and strained through a cloth. With 1 qt. of raspberry juice, use 2 lbs. of sugar and 2 qts. of white wine and let it come to a boil. Cool it and fill into bottles that are well corked and kept in a cool place.

No. 15—PEACH PUNCH.

3 lbs. of peaches
½ lb. of sugar
2 bottles of white wine
1 bottle of red wine

Preparation: The peaches are peeled and sliced, put into a bowl with sugar, ¼ bottle of white wine and let stand 3 to 4 hours. Then pour on the rest of the white wine and red wine and serve very cold.

No. 16—MAY BOWL OR WOODRUFF PUNCH.

2 bottles of white wine
About 1/20 lb. of woodruff
¼ lb. of sugar

Preparation: One-half bottle of white wine is poured on the woodruff. Cover the bowl and let stand several hours. Then add the rest of the wine and sugar. Place the bowl on ice.

Remarks: This May bowl may be improved by mixing a bottle of champagne and 1 cupful of strawberries with it when serving.

No. 17—CURRANT WINE.

10 qts. of currant juice
20 qts. of water
15 lbs. of sugar
1 qt. corn brandy

Preparation: Red and white currants are mashed and strained through a cloth. To 10 qts. of juice, add 15 lbs. of sugar and 20 qts. of water. Put it into a clean cask, and leave it to ferment for 3 weeks. After that time empty the cask, clean it well, then pour back the wine and leave it two weeks longer, then add the brandy. Now close up the cask tightly and place it so that it need not be moved when the wine is drawn off. Bottle the wine after six months, without moving the cask.

No. 18—WARMBEER.

1 qt. beer
Sugar to taste
A piece of butter the size of an egg
½ pt. of milk
3 yolks of eggs
1 piece of cinnamon

Preparation: Beer, sugar and butter are brought to boil; then milk and yolks of eggs are mixed well and added; season with cinnamon, let all come to a boil and serve hot.

No. 19—COLD LEMONADE.

1 qt. of cold water
Juice of 1 lemon
¾ cup of sugar

Preparation: Dissolve the sugar in the water, add the lemon juice, mix well and serve very cold.

No. 20—FINE LEMONADE.

1 qt. of cold water
Sugar
Juice of 1 orange
2 bananas
Juice of ½ lemon

Preparation: Dissolve the sugar in the water, mix in the lemon and orange juice and pour the whole over the sliced bananas.

No. 21—ALMOND MILK.

½ lb. sweet almonds
1¼ qts. of water
Scant ½ lb. of sugar
4 tbsps. of rose water

Preparation: The almonds are blanched and ground, then put into a porcelain dish. Add the water and sugar and let stand 20 minutes, then strain through a cloth and add the rose water.

No. 22—CHOCOLATE.

Quantity for 6 Persons.

½ lb. of chocolate
½ cup of water
Sugar to taste
1½ qts. of milk

Preparation: The chocolate is broken into pieces and dissolved in the water on the stove, the milk is added and brought to boil. Mix in sugar to suit your taste.

Remarks: You may stir in 2 yolks of eggs. Plain chocolate is made by using more water and mixing 1 tablespoonful of flour with water and adding this to the chocolate while cooking.

No. 23—ICE CHOCOLATE.

Ingredients and preparation are the same as given under No. 22, Chocolate. When cooled off, strain through a sieve, add 1 teaspoonful of vanilla, place into ice and salt for 3 hours and serve in tumblers or sherbet cups with whipped cream on top.

No. 24—COCOA.

Quantity for 6 Persons.

4 tbsps. of cocoa
1½ qts. of milk
½ tsp. of vanilla
Sugar to taste
2 yolks of eggs

Preparation: The cocoa is stirred smooth with milk, add the sugar, let it get hot, stirring constantly. Add the rest of the milk, cook 1 minute and add the vanilla. Mix the yolks of eggs well with one tablespoonful of milk and stir into the cocoa.

Remarks: You may omit the yolks of eggs and instead stir a tablespoonful of flour, mixed with water, into the boiling cocoa.

No. 25—TEA.

Enough for 12 cups.

8 even tsps. of tea

2 qts. of water

Preparation: The tea is put into a well covered pot. Pour on 1 pt. of boiling water, cover and let it steep 3 minutes, then pour on the rest of the water and set to draw again 5 minutes before serving.

No. 26—TEA WITH VANILLA.

Ingredients and preparation are the same as given under No. 25, Tea. But add to this ½ teaspoonful of vanilla.

Remarks: You may add a small piece of lemon peel when pouring on the water.

Dried tea leaves may be used for sweeping carpets. Moisten the leaves and sprinkle them on the carpet. This will clean the carpet and absorb the dust when sweeping.

No. 27—ICED TEA.

The ingredients and preparation are the same as given under No. 25, Tea. After the tea has steeped long enough, pour it off, cool it and put in pieces of clean ice, sugar and into each glass 1 to 2 slices of lemon.

No. 28—COFFEE.

Enough for 12 cups.

6 tbsps. of ground coffee
14 cups of boiling water

Preparation: It is best to grind the coffee fresh and fine every time you wish to make some. The water must boil when you pour it on. Close the pot well.

Remarks: There are various ways of making coffee. A. An egg may be stirred into the ground coffee before pouring on the hot water. B. It may be made in a machine in which the water boils and little water gets onto the coffee at a time. This is the best way. C. Pour the hot water on the coffee, simmer 5 minutes and strain. This is the quickest way of making coffee.

No. 29—GOOSEBERRY OR CURRANT WINE.

For a 6 gallon cask use 18 lbs. of sugar
3–4 gallons of juice
Water to fill the cask

Clean and pick over the berries, wash them and press out the juice well. The cask must be very clean and odorless. Scald it several times and then dry it in the fresh air, put in the sugar and enough water to dissolve it while shaking the cask. When the sugar is dissolved, add the strained juice. Place the cask into a place like the garret where it is warm. It will soon ferment, then remove the foam from the bunghole every morning, stir the wine with a clean wooden stick and fill in fresh water so the cask remains full. After about 6 weeks the fermenting will cease, then close the bunghole with a cork, leave it in the cask another 3 to 4 months and then put the wine into bottles. Cork and seal them well and set them upright in the cellar, where it is dark and cold.

BREAD AND CAKES.

No. 1—WHEAT BREAD No. 1.

Enough for 2 Loaves.

8 cups of wheat flour
1½ cents' worth of yeast
1 pt. of milk
1 pt. of water
2 tbsps. of salt

Preparation: The 4 cups of flour are put into a mixing bowl, lukewarm milk and wafer added and mixed into a smooth batter. The yeast is dissolved and stirred in ¼ cup of milk and mixed into the batter; sprinkle a little flour over it and put the sponge in a warm place to rise. If the pan is ¼ full, it, must rise to half fill the pan. Put in the salt and the rest of the flour, knead the dough for 15 minutes and put into two greased bread pans to rise again. If the pans are half full, the bread must rise to the brim of the pan. Brush the top of the bread with cold water and bake it in medium hot oven for 45 minutes.

No. 2—WHEAT BREAD No. 2.

Enough for 2 Loaves.

8 cups of flour
1½ cents' worth of yeast
1 qt. of milk
2 tbsps. of salt
1 tbsp. of lard

The preparation is the same as given under No. 1. When the second part of the flour is kneaded into the dough, work in 1 tablespoonful of lard.

Remarks: You may take butter instead of lard. One cup of boiled and grated potatoes may be mixed with the flour.

No. 3—RYE BREAD WITH LEAVEN.

Enough for 2 Loaves.

11 cups of rye flour
1 qt. of water
3 cents' worth of leaven
2 tbsps. of salt
1 tsp. of caraway seed if you like

Preparation: Mix 4 cups of flour with lukewarm water, then add the leaven or yeast, strew a little flour over and set to rise to double its bulk. Then knead in the salt and caraway seed and the rest of the flour and continue kneading for 20 minutes. Make two loaves and put them into greased pans and set to rise again to twice its size, brush it with cold water and bake 1 hour.

No. 4—RYE BREAD WITH YEAST.

Enough for 2 Loaves.

11 cups of rye flour
1 qt. of water
2 cents' worth of yeast.
1 tsp. of caraway seed if desired
2 tbsps. of salt

The preparation is the same as given under No. 3, using yeast instead of leaven. Dissolve the yeast in ¼ cup of lukewarm water and mix it with the flour.

No. 5—HEALTH BREAD OR GROATS BREAD.

Enough for 2 Loaves.

8–9 cups of coarse meal or flour (groats)
1 qt. of water
2 cents' worth of yeast.
1½ tbsps. of salt

Preparation: Sift 4 cups of flour and mix it to a smooth batter with lukewarm water and yeast that is dissolved in ¼ cup of water, then set the sponge to rise. After this mix in the salt and knead the rest of the flour in and continue kneading 20 minutes. Form two loaves and put them into greased pans, then set them to rise again to twice their size. Bake ¾ to 1 hour in medium hot oven.

No. 6—BREAD STICKS.

Quantity for 6 Persons.

Ingredients and preparation are given under Chapter 1, Soups, No. 16, Bread Sticks.

No. 7—BISCUIT.

Quantity for 10 Persons.

4½ cups of flour
1 pt. of milk
1½ cents' worth of yeast
¼ lb. of butter
1 egg
½ tsp. of salt

Preparation: Mix 2 cups of flour to a smooth batter with the lukewarm milk and the yeast dissolved in ¼ cup the lukewarm milk, then set to rise in a warm place. Mix in the melted butter, egg and salt and beat the batter 20 minutes, then add the rest of the flour. Roll out the dough to about ¾ inch thickness, cut out biscuits with a tumbler, fold them half over or leave them round, put them into floured or greased tins, set to rise and bake them to a nice color.

Remarks: If you wish sweet biscuits, stir in ½ cup of sugar. The dough must be beaten 20 minutes.

No. 8—COFFEE CAKE.

Enough for 2 Cakes.

3½–4 cups of flour
1 pt. of milk
¼ lb. of butter
¼ lb. of sugar
3 eggs
1 cent yeast
½ grated lemon rind

Preparation: The milk is made lukewarm and stirred to a smooth batter with 2¼ cups of flour, then the yeast dissolved in ¼ cup of lukewarm, milk is mixed in quickly and put in a warm place to rise. After the sponge has risen well, mix in the melted butter, sugar, grated lemon rind, the eggs and the rest of the flour, stir the dough thoroughly with a spoon. Butter 2 tins and put in the dough about 1 inch thick, then set to rise; after this strew on sugar, cinnamon and put on small pieces of butter and some chopped almonds. Bake in medium hot oven.

No. 9—STREUSEL COFFEE CAKE.

Preparation of the Streusel.

A piece of butter the size of an egg
½ cup of flour

1¼ cups of sugar
½ cup of ground almonds
Yeast dough like No. 8
1 tsp. of cinnamon

Preparation: The dough is prepared as given under No. 8, Coffee Cake. Instead of strewing on sugar, cinnamon and pieces of butter, you make sugar crumbs as follows: Melt the butter, mix flour, sugar, cinnamon and almonds with it and rub to crumbs with the hands. Sprinkle over the cakes before baking.

No. 10—SCHNECKEN (SNAILS).

Yeast dough like No. 8

For the Filling.

⅛ lb. of butter
1 cup of sugar
½ cup of blanched, ground almonds
1 cup of currants

Preparation: The preparation is the same as given under No. 8, Coffee Cake. Stir in 1 cup of flour more than given in No. 8, roll out the dough to 1 inch thickness, strew it with sugar, cinnamon, currants, almonds, sprinkle with melted butter, roll it up carefully and cut slices off to make the snails. Place these into a buttered tin and set to rise about ½ hour. Then bake them in a medium hot oven, brush them while hot with melted butter and sprinkle with sugar.

No. 11—FILLED BERLINER PANCAKES OR STUFFED DOUGHNUTS.

Yeast dough, according to No. 8

Lard for baking
Jelly for filling

Preparation: The dough is prepared like No. 8, Coffee Cake, but 1 cup of flour more is kneaded in than given under No. 8. Roll out the dough ½ inch thick, cut out small disks with a tumbler, put on one disk some jelly or thick apple sauce, place another disk on top and fasten the two by pressing the dough together all around, leave them on a floured board or tin and set to rise. Heat the lard in an iron kettle and put in a few Berliners at a time and bake them golden yellow. They must be fried in deep fat. Prick them with a knitting needle to see whether the dough is baked enough. While hot, roll them in sugar.

No. 12—WREATH CAKE.

1 lb. of flour
¾ cup of butter
4 eggs
1½ cents yeast
2 tbsps. of vanilla
½ cup of milk
¼ lb. of sugar

Preparation: Cream the butter, stir in the eggs, sugar vanilla, the yeast which has been dissolved in ½ cup of lukewarm milk and the flour. Roll out the dough quite thick, cut three strips of it and braid it. Then make a wreath of this braid and put it into a buttered pan to rise in a warm place. Brush it with yolks of eggs, strew sugar on and bake in a hot oven to a nice color.

No. 13—ROUND COFFEE CAKE No. 1.

1 lb. of flour
½ lb. of butter
½ lb. of sugar

½ lemon peel
1½ cents yeast
3 eggs
1 cup of milk

Preparation: Cream the butter with sugar and eggs. The yeast is dissolved in 1 cup of lukewarm milk and mixed in, also the grated ½ lemon peel; then stir in the flour and beat the dough well for 20 minutes. Butter a round cake pan with tube, fill in the dough to half full and let it rise in a warm place to the top of the pan. Then bake it 1 hour.

No. 14—ROUND COFFEE CAKE WITH RAISINS.

4 cups of flour
1 pt. of milk
3 eggs
Scant ½ lb. of butter
½ lemon peel
1 cup of sugar
1 cup of raisins
2 cents yeast

Preparation: Let the milk get lukewarm and stir to a smooth batter with 2¼ cups of flour, mix with the yeast dissolved in ¼ cup of lukewarm milk. Set the sponge to rise in a warm place, then stir in the melted butter, eggs, sugar, grated lemon peel, raisins and the rest of the flour, beat this dough well for 10 minutes. Butter a round cake pan with tube, fill it half full and set to rise in a warm place until the pan is full, then bake to a nice color for ¾ to 1 hour.

No. 15—STOLLEN.
Sufficient for 2–3 Cakes.

1 qt. of milk

6 cents yeast
12 to 15 cups of flour
1 lb. of sugar
1 lb. of butter
6 eggs
¼ lb. of blanched, ground almonds
⅛ lb. of bitter, blanched, ground almonds
¼ cup of brandy
1½ lbs. of raisins
¼ lb. of cut citron

Preparation: Warm the milk and stir into a smooth batter with 4½ cups of flour, add the yeast dissolved in ½ cup of lukewarm milk and set the sponge to rise. Stir in the melted butter, sugar, eggs, raisins, citron, sweet and bitter almonds, brandy and the rest of the flour to make a pretty stiff dough. Knead it until it will not adhere to the hands. Cut the dough into 2 or 3 parts, as many "stollen" as you wish to have, and shape them nice and round, then set to rise in a warm place. Butter a pan for each cake, double up the dough, place it into the pan and set to rise again. Bake in a medium oven. If the cakes are large, bake them 2 hours, if small, 1½ hours. As soon as you take them out of the oven, brush them with butter and strew them with sugar. These cakes must be prepared in a warm place.

No. 16—APPLE CAKE.

Yeast dough like No. 8
Sweet-sour apples
Sugar
Cinnamon

For Frosting.

½ cup of cream
2 eggs
¼ cup of sugar

Preparation: The dough is prepared like No. 8, Coffee Cake. Butter some pans and spread the dough out in them ¼ inch thick, then set to rise in a warm place.

Peel and slice the apples, place them on the dough in rows, sprinkle with sugar and cinnamon, then bake. After the cake is baked, spread the frosting on. The frosting is made by mixing cream, yolks of eggs, sugar and beaten whites of eggs; spread it on the cakes and bake them 10 minutes longer.

Remarks: The frosting is sufficient for 1 small cake. The dough will make 4 to 5 cakes, according to size.

No. 17—CHERRY CAKE.

Yeast dough like No. 8
Stoned sweet-sour cherries
Sugar
Frosting like No. 16

Preparation: The dough is prepared like No. 8, Coffee Cake. Put the dough, about ½ inch thick, into buttered pans and set to rise in a warm place. The cherries and the sugar are put on thick, then the cake is baked in a hot oven. After taking it out, spread on the frosting which has been prepared according to No. 16, Apple Cake, and bake 10 minutes longer. This cake may be prepared without the frosting.

No. 18—PLUM CAKE.

Yeast dough like No. 8
Stoned plums
Sugar
Frosting like No. 16

The preparation is the same as given under No. 17.

No. 19—CHEESE CAKE.

Feast dough like No. 8
1½ lbs. cottage cheese
½ pt. of cream
¼ lb. of sugar
3 eggs
½ tsp. of vanilla
1 pinch of salt
⅛ lb. of butter

Preparation: The dough is prepared according to No. 8. Butter some pans, spread the dough out in them ¼ inch thick and set to rise. During this time prepare the cheese. The cottage cheese, cream, sugar, eggs, salt and vanilla are mixed well and spread over the dough quite thick. The butter is melted and sprinkled over the cheese, then the cake is baked to a nice color.

Remarks: You may mix into the cheese ½ cup of currants.

No. 20—CURRANT CAKE.

Yeast dough like No. 8
Currants
Sugar
Frosting like No. 16

The preparation and baking are just the same as given under No. 17, Cherry Cake.

No. 21—POPPY SEED CAKE.

Yeast dough like No. 8
2 lbs. of poppy seed
3 juicy pears
¼ lb. of sugar

3 eggs
⅛ lb. of butter

Preparation: The dough is prepared according to No. 8 and spread out in buttered pans about ¼ inch thick, then set to rise in a warm place. The poppy seed is scalded and the water drained off. The pears are peeled and grated into the poppy seed, sugar and eggs are mixed in. Spread the poppy seed mixture thick on the dough, sprinkle melted butter on and bake ¾ hour.

No. 22—HUCKLEBERRY CAKE.

Yeast dough like No. 8
Huckleberries
Sugar
Frosting according to No. 16

Preparation: The dough is prepared as given under No. 8, spread out in buttered pans about ¼ inch thick, then set to rise in a warm place. The berries are strewn on thick and sprinkled with sugar. Bake it and if you wish, spread the frosting on according to No. 16.

No. 23—ONION CAKE.

Yeast dough like No. 8
6 peeled onions
2 sweet-sour apples
¼ lb. of sugar
¼ lb. of butter

Preparation: The dough is prepared as given under No. 8, spread out in buttered pans about ¼ inch thick and set to rise in a warm place. The onions are peeled, sliced and stewed a little in ⅛ lb. of butter, to which the peeled and finely chopped apples are added. Strew sugar on the dough and spread on the onions mixed with apples ¼ inch thick, sprinkle with sugar, then with the melted butter and bake to a nice golden color.

Remarks: The apples may be omitted.

No. 24—COFFEE CAKE WITH EGG CREAM.

Yeast dough like No. 8
½ lb. of butter
11 eggs
¾ lb. of sugar

Preparation: The dough is prepared as given under No. 8, rolled out to ¼ inch thickness and put into buttered pans to rise in a warm place. Melt the butter and stir with the eggs to a thick cream. This cream is spread thickly on the dough and the cake baked quickly in a hot oven. When the cake is done, put on quite a little butter and sprinkle with plenty of sugar.

Baking Powder Cakes.

No. 25—COFFEE CAKE WITH ALMOND FROSTING.

½ cup of butter
1½ cups of sugar
1 cup of milk
3 cups of flour
4 eggs
Juice and rind of 1 lemon
2 heaping tsps. of baking powder

For the Frosting.

1 cup of almonds

¼ cup of melted butter
1 cup of sugar
1 tsp. of cinnamon

Preparation: Cream the butter, stir in sugar, lemon juice and rind, gradually mix in yolks of eggs, milk and flour. Lastly add the baking powder and the beaten whites of eggs. Spread this batter out 1 inch thick into buttered pans, sprinkle with sugar, cinnamon and blanched almonds cut into narrow strips, sprinkle butter over and bake to a nice color.

No. 26—COFFEE CAKE WITH CHOCOLATE FROSTING.

The batter according to No. 25
¼ lb. of chocolate
⅛ lb. of sugar
1 tsp. of vanilla
3 tbsps. of cold water
1 white of egg

Preparation: The batter is prepared and baked as in No. 25. Dissolve the chocolate over the fire in the water, add sugar and vanilla and stir until it becomes stringy. Now mix the beaten whites of eggs with it and spread on the cake when it is baked.

No. 27—ROUND COFFEE CAKE No. 2.

Ingredients and preparation are given under No. 25. Put the batter into a round cake pan with tube and bake it ½ hour.

No. 28—STIRRED CAKE.

¾ cup of butter

1¼ cups of powdered sugar
2 cups of flour
Juice of ½ lemon
1½ tsps. of baking powder
6 whites of eggs

Preparation: Cream the butter and mix with sugar, lemon juice and flour, add 1½ teaspoonfuls of baking powder and the beaten whites of eggs. Put in a buttered pan and bake ½ to ¾ hour.

No. 29—LAYER CAKE WITH CHOCOLATE.

½ lb. of butter
½ lb. of sugar
6 eggs
½ lb. of flour
2 heaping tsps. of baking powder
¼ lb. of chocolate

For the Filling.

½ cup of cream
3 eggs
1½ tsps. of vanilla
4 tbsps. of sugar

Preparation: Cream the butter, then mix with sugar, yolks of eggs, flour, and lastly the baking powder and beaten whites of eggs. The chocolate is grated and mixed with one-half of the batter. Bake in four layers, 2 light or yellow ones and 2 dark ones containing chocolate.

The filling is made by mixing well: cream, yolks of eggs, vanilla and sugar and cooking it in a double boiler to a thick cream, stirring constantly. Let it get cold, mix with the beaten whites of eggs and spread it between the layers, putting them together light and dark alternately. The cake may be covered with a chocolate frosting.

No. 30—LAYER CAKE WITH JELLY FILLING.

½ lb. of butter
½ lb. of sugar
5 eggs
½ lb. of flour
2 heaping tsps. of baking powder
Jelly for the filling

Preparation: Cream the butter with sugar, add the yolks of eggs, then gradually work in the flour, baking powder and beaten whites of eggs. Bake in three layers and when these are cooled off, spread jelly over them and place one on the other. If you like, cover the cake with a white frosting.

No. 31—LAYER CAKE WITH BANANA FILLING.

1 cup of butter
2 cups of sugar
2½ cups of flour
6 eggs
½ cup of milk
2 heaping tsps. of baking powder

For the Filling.

4–5 peeled and sliced bananas
¼ cup of sugar

Preparation: Cream the butter with the sugar and yolks of eggs; gradually add the milk and the flour, and lastly the baking powder and beaten whites of eggs. Bake in 4 layers and when these are cooled, spread the sugared, sliced bananas between the layers and cover the cake with white frosting.

No. 32—LAYER CAKE WITH COCOANUT FILLING.
No. 1.

1 cup of butter
2 cups of sugar
4 yolks of eggs
2 whites of eggs
1 cup of milk
2½ cups of flour
2 heaping tsps. of baking powder

For the Filling.

¼ lb. of cocoanut
2 whites of eggs
½ cup of sugar
1 tsp. of vanilla

Preparation: Cream the butter with the sugar, add yolks of eggs and the milk and gradually stir in the flour. Lastly add the baking powder and beaten whites of eggs. Bake in three layers and prepare the filling in the meantime. Mix the beaten whites of eggs with sugar, cocoanut and vanilla and spread between the layers as well as on and over the whole cake.

No. 33—SPONGE CAKE.

4 eggs
1 cup of sugar
5 tsps. of milk
1 tsp. of vanilla or lemon juice
1 cup of flour
1 pinch of salt
1 heaping tsp. of baking powder

For the Filling.

½ cup of milk
4 tbsps. of sugar
1 tsp. of vanilla or essence of lemon
2 eggs
1 tsp. of flour

Preparation: Cream the sugar and yolks of eggs and add milk, vanilla and ½ cup of flour. To the beaten whites of eggs stir ½ cup of flour and mix it with the rest, then add salt and baking powder. Bake in two layers and prepare the filling in the meantime. Milk, yolks of eggs, sugar and vanilla are mixed well and cooked to a thick cream in a double boiler, stirring constantly. When this is cooled off, mix in the beaten whites of eggs and spread the filling between the layers. Put a cocoanut frosting on the cake.

No. 34—GOLD CAKE.

1 cup of butter
2 cups of sugar
6 yolks of eggs
1 tsp. of vanilla to taste
1 cup of milk
3½ cups of flour
1½ heaping tsps. of baking powder

Preparation: Cream the butter and mix with sugar, yolks of eggs and vanilla, then add milk and gradually the flour and lastly the baking powder. Butter a cake pan, fill in the dough and bake 1 hour.

No. 35—SILVER CAKE.

½ cup of butter
1½ cups of sugar
1 tbsp. of vanilla
1 cup of milk

1½ cups of flour
½ cup of corn starch
2 heaping tsps. of baking powder
6 whites of eggs

Preparation: Cream the butter and sugar, add vanilla, milk, gradually the corn starch, then baking powder and lastly the beaten whites of eggs. Put into a buttered pan and bake 1 hour.

No. 36—THEATER CAKE.

1 tbsp. of butter
2 cups of sugar
1 egg
1 tsp. of lemon essence or vanilla
1 cup of milk
1¾ cups of flour
1½ tsps. of baking powder

Preparation: Cream the butter with sugar, yolks of eggs and vanilla; add the milk, then flour, baking powder and the beaten whites of eggs. Put into a buttered pan and bake ½ hour.

No. 37—FLAT CAKE.

1 lb. of butter
1 lb. of sugar
8 eggs
Juice of 2 lemons
1½ lemon peels
A little cardamom
2 lbs. of flour
1 heaping tsp. of salt of hartshorn

Preparation: The butter is melted, yolks of eggs and sugar are put in and stirred to a cream. Add the grated lemon peel and juice, cardamom and gradually work in the flour. Mix the salt of hartshorn with a little flour and stir it in. Lastly mix in the well-beaten whites of eggs and spread the dough out in buttered pans about 2 inches thick. Sprinkle with sugar, cinnamon and ground almonds and bake to a nice color.

No. 38—POTATO CAKE OR TART.

1 lb. boiled, peeled, grated potatoes
14 eggs
1 lb. of sugar
Juice and rind of 2 lemons
½ lb. blanched, ground almonds

Preparation: The yolks of eggs and sugar are beaten to a cream; then grated lemon rind and juice, the ground almonds, potatoes and beaten whites of eggs mixed in. Butter a round, loose bottom pan and strew with bread crumbs, put the batter in and bake slowly for 1 to 1½ hours.

Remarks: Tarts, so-called in Europe, differ very much from the dainties similarly designated in this country. The former are more like our American pies, but without an upper crust. Sometimes they have narrow strips of crust laid in the form of lattice work across the top.

No. 39—RICE CAKE OR TART.

1 lb. of rice
2½ qts. of milk
12 eggs
½ lb. of butter
½ lb. of sugar
1 lb. of raisins
1 tsp. of cinnamon

Preparation: The rice is washed and partly cooked in milk, but do not stir it, for the kernels must stay whole. Cool the rice. Cream the butter and sugar, add raisins and cinnamon, then the rice and lastly the beaten whites of eggs. Butter a round, loose bottom cake pan, strew with bread crumbs, put the batter in and bake slowly.

No. 40—STRAWBERRY SHORT CAKE.

½ cup of butter
½ cup of sugar
½ cup of milk
3 eggs
2 cups of flour
2 heaping tsps. of baking powder

For the Filling.

2–3 qts. of strawberries
1 pt. of whipped cream
Sugar to taste
1 tsp. of vanilla

Preparation: Cream the butter with sugar, yolks of eggs and milk, gradually work in the flour and baking powder and lastly the beaten whites of eggs. The dough is baked in 2 layers, each being 1½ inches thick. When they are cool, spread between the layers and on top crushed strawberries mixed with sugar and on this the whipped cream mixed with sugar and vanilla.

Remarks: After the whipped cream is on the strawberry short cake, it must be served at once.

No. 41—DEVIL'S FOOD.
For the First Half.

½ cup of butter
½ cup of milk
1 cup of brown sugar
2 cups of flour
1 egg
2 yolks of eggs
1 tsp. of soda

For the Second Half.

1 cup of brown sugar
½ cup of milk
1 cup of grated bitter chocolate

For the Filling.

The cream prepared according to [No. 29]()

Preparation: The first half is prepared by creaming the butter, mixing with sugar, egg and yolks of eggs. Dissolve the soda in milk and stir it into the mixture, then measure and sift the flour and add it gradually.

The second half is prepared by putting the brown sugar, the bitter chocolate and milk into a double boiler, to stew to a smooth cream which is set to cool. Now the first and second half are put together, mixed and baked in three layers. When these are cooled, make the cream according to No. 29, see Layer Cake with Chocolate, and spread between the layers. Cover the cake with a chocolate frosting.

No. 42—ANGEL'S FOOD.

9 whites of eggs
1 tsp. of cream of tartar
1 cup of sugar
1 cup of the finest flour
1 tsp. of vanilla

Preparation: The whites of eggs are beaten to a stiff froth, the cream of tartar stirred in and also the sugar and vanilla. The flour is sifted 7 times and at last mixed with the other ingredients. Put into a buttered pan and bake slowly ½ hour.

No. 43—YELLOW ANGEL'S FOOD.

12 ounces of sugar
5 ounces of fine flour
1 tsp. of cream of tartar
11 whites of eggs
6 yolks of eggs
1 tsp. of vanilla

Preparation: The sugar is sifted 4 times and stirred to a cream with yolks of eggs; add the beaten whites of eggs, cream of tartar and vanilla. Sift the flour 5 times and work it in. Put the batter into a buttered pan and bake slowly ¾ to 1 hour.

No. 44—FIG CAKE.

¾ cup of butter
2 cups of sugar
6 whites of eggs
1 cup of milk
2 cups of flour
½ cup of corn starch
12 figs
3 heaping tsps. of baking powder
1 tsp. of cinnamon
1 tsp. of cloves

For the Frosting.

3 whites of eggs
1 tbsp. of sugar
4 tbsps. of water
½ lb. finely chopped almonds

Preparation: Cream the butter, add the sugar, milk, flour, baking powder and lastly the beaten whites of eggs. Divide the batter into 3 parts. Into the first part mix the cinnamon, cloves and chopped figs. Bake two light and one dark layer and arrange them with the dark layer in the middle. Prepare the frosting by beating the whites of eggs to a stiff froth and mixing it with 1 tablespoonful of sugar and 4 tablespoonfuls of water which have been boiled 5 minutes. The mixture is stirred until cool, the almonds are added and the frosting spread over the cake.

No. 45—LAYER CAKE WITH COCOANUT. No. 2.

⅔ cup of butter
2 cups of sugar
1 cup of flour
2 heaping tsps. of baking powder
7 whites of eggs

For the Filling.

Cream according to No. 29.

For the Frosting.

4 whites of eggs
½ cup of sugar
¼ lb. of cocoanut

Preparation: Cream the butter with sugar, then add flour and baking powder and the beaten whites of eggs. Bake in 4 layers. Make the filling according to No. 29, Layer Cake With Chocolate, and when the layers are cool, spread the cream between them. Make the frosting from the beaten whites of eggs mixed with sugar, spread it on the cake and sprinkle with grated cocoanut.

No. 46—TEA CAKE.

½ lb. of sugar
10 eggs
½ lb. of fine flour
¼ lb. of blanched, grated almonds
Juice and rind of 1 lemon
2 heaping tsps. of baking powder

Preparation: The sugar and yolks of eggs are stirred 20 minutes, the ground almonds added and the mixture stirred again 20 minutes. Now add lemon juice and grated lemon rind, the whites of eggs beaten to a froth, and then quickly stir in the flour. Lastly add the baking powder mixed with some of the flour. Put the batter into a buttered pan and bake 1 hour.

Remarks: In the beginning, the heat may be greater in the bottom of the oven than in the top.

No. 47—SUNSHINE CAKE.

5 eggs
1 cup of sugar
¼ tsp. of salt
¾ cup of flour
½ tsp. of cream of tartar
1 tsp. of lemon juice
1 tsp. of orange juice

Preparation: The yolks of eggs are stirred with sugar ½ hour. The flour mixed with the cream of tartar is sifted 4 times. Add salt, lemon and orange juice, the sifted flour and the whites of eggs beaten to a froth. Butter a pan and strew it with roll crumbs, put the batter in and bake 40 minutes in medium hot oven.

No. 48—FRUIT CAKE.

1 lb. of butter
1 lb. of brown sugar
12 eggs
1½ lbs. of flour
6 tbsps. of molasses
2 tsps. of soda
4 lbs. of Sultana raisins
3 lbs. of small raisins
1 lb. of chopped citron
1 chopped orange rind
½ lb. of chopped figs
½ pt. of brandy
¼ pt. of white wine
¼ pt. of rose water
½ tsp. ground cloves
¼ tsp. mace and nutmeg

Preparation: Cream the butter with sugar and yolks of eggs. Dissolve soda in molasses and mix it into the batter, add the brandy, white wine, rose water, ground cloves, mace, nutmeg, flour and lastly the beaten whites of eggs. Mix in the Sultana and the small raisins, citron, orange rind and figs. Line a pan with buttered paper, put the batter in and bake slowly for 2 hours.

No. 49—BREMER BLOCK.

1 lb. washed butter
¾ lb. of sugar
1 lb. of seeded raisins

¾ lb. of currants
¼ lb. blanched, chopped almonds
¼ lb. of chopped citron
¾ qt. warm milk
5 cents yeast
3 tsps. of salt
3 lbs. of sifted flour

Preparation: Cream the butter and sugar. Wash the raisins and currants and put them in a warm place; when real warm, mix them with the butter. Almonds and citron are next stirred in, then the warm milk, the yeast dissolved in ½ cup of warm milk, salt and flour. Put the dough into buttered pans, set to rise and bake 1½ to 2 hours.

No. 50—PLAIN FRUIT CAKE.

1 cup of butter
1 cup of brown sugar
1 cup of white sugar
1 cup of raisins
1 cup of currants
½ cup of molasses
1½ cups of black coffee
3 eggs
4 cups of flour
3 tsps. of saleratus

Preparation: Cream the butter with sugar and yolks of eggs, add raisins, currants and saleratus dissolved in molasses; then coffee, flour and lastly whites of eggs beaten to a stiff froth. Put the batter into a pan lined with buttered paper and bake in a moderate oven 1 to 1½ hours.

No. 51—BROWN SPICE CAKE No. 1.

2 eggs
2 heaping tbsps. of lard
1 lb. best molasses
1 lb. of brown sugar
1 tsp. of ground cloves
1 tsp. of cinnamon
1 cup of raisins
1 pinch of salt
1 level tsp. baking soda
1 heaping tsp. of cream of tartar
1 cup of sour milk or black coffee
4 cups of flour
½ grated nutmeg

Preparation: The eggs are beaten thoroughly, lard heated a little, sugar, molasses, cloves, cinnamon, nutmeg, raisins and salt mixed in. The soda is dissolved in the milk or coffee and added. The cream of tartar is mixed into the flour, and this added gradually. Line a pan with buttered paper, put the batter in and bake 1 to 1½ hours in medium hot oven.

No. 52—NATRON OR CARBONATE OF SODA CAKE.

¼ lb. of butter
2 cups of sugar
1 cup milk
5 eggs
Juice and rind of 1 lemon
10 bitter almonds
1 lb. of flour
1½ tsps. of cream of tartar
1 tsp. of natron, (carbonate of soda)
⅛ lb. of sweet almonds

Preparation: Cream the butter, sugar and yolks of eggs, then add lemon juice and grated rind and the blanched, ground sweet and bitter almonds. The carbonate of soda and cream of tartar are mixed into the flour and this is gradually worked into the batter; and lastly, stir in lightly the stiffly beaten whites of eggs. Put into a buttered pan and bake 1 hour.

No. 53—LIGHTNING CAKE.

½ lb. of sugar
4 eggs
½ lb. of butter
1 grated lemon rind
½ lb. of flour
2 tsps. of baking powder

For Sprinkling on the Cake.

¼ lb. blanched, ground almonds
½ cup of sugar
1 tsp. of cinnamon

Preparation: Cream the butter, sugar and yolks of eggs, add the lemon rind, flour mixed with baking powder and lastly the stiffly beaten whites of eggs. Butter some pans, spread the dough out in them about ⅛ inch thick, sprinkle with almonds, sugar and cinnamon. Bake in medium oven and while still warm, cut into nice pieces and serve warm.

No. 54—CARAWAY CAKE.

½ lb. of butter
¾ cup of sugar
1 lb. of flour
¼ lb. of raisins
3 eggs
½ pt. of milk
1 tbsp. of caraway
1 tsp. of natron or soda

Preparation: The butter and flour are rubbed together, raisins, sugar and caraway and the well-beaten eggs stirred in. Boil the milk and dissolve the soda in it, let it get cold and stir into the dough. Put the batter into a buttered pan and bake ¾ to 1 hour.

No. 55—WIT CAKE.

6 eggs
¾ lb. of sugar
½ lb. of flour
Juice of ½ lemon
2 tbsps. of arrack
1½ tsps. of baking powder
¼ lb. of butter

For Sprinkling.

¼ lb. of chopped, blanched almonds

Preparation: Stir the yolks of eggs and sugar to a cream, work in the flour. Add the melted butter, arrack, lemon juice, baking powder and beaten whites of eggs. Butter some pans, spread the batter in 1 inch thick, sprinkle the almonds over and bake the cake ½ hour.

No. 56—ENGLISH CAKE.

¼ lb. of butter
¾ lb. of flour
Scarce ½ lb. of sugar
⅛ lb. of raisins
2 tbsps. of chopped orange rind
4 eggs
½ pt. of milk
4 grams of ammonium
2 tbsps. of chopped citron

Preparation: Butter, flour and sugar are rubbed together with the hands. Add to this the raisins, citron, grated orange rind; beat the 4 eggs to a froth, boil the milk and mix it with the eggs, then stir into the batter and lastly mix in the ammonium. Butter a pan, strew it with roll crumbs, fill in the batter and bake in medium hot oven 1 hour.

No. 57—WALNUT CAKE.

½ cup of butter
1 cup of brown sugar
2 eggs
1 cup of sour milk
½ cup of chopped walnuts
½ cup of chopped raisins
2 cups of flour

2 tsps. of baking powder
½ tsp. of soda

Preparation: Cream the butter, add sugar and eggs and beat 10 minutes. Soda is dissolved in sour milk and mixed into the batter, the walnuts, raisins, flour and lastly the baking powder added. Put the batter into buttered pans and bake to a nice color.

No. 58—SPICE CAKE No. 2.

1 cup of butter
1½ cups of sugar
1 cup of sour milk
1 tsp. of soda
3 eggs
2 cups of raisins
2 tsps. of cinnamon
1 tsp. of cloves
½ tsp. of nutmeg
2 cups of flour

Preparation: Cream the butter with sugar and yolks of eggs, then add soda, dissolved in sour milk, and raisins, cinnamon, ground cloves, nutmeg and flour, and lastly the whites of eggs beaten to a stiff froth. Butter a pan, put in the batter and bake 1 hour.

No. 59—SOUR CREAM CAKE.

1 cup of sugar
1 cup of sour milk
1 egg
1 pinch of salt
1 pinch of nutmeg
1 tsp. of soda

1 cup of flour

Preparation: The soda is mixed with sour milk and to it are added in the order named, sugar, yolk of egg, salt, nutmeg, flour and the stiffly beaten white of egg. Bake the batter in two layers and spread on the lower layer the sour cream filling. This is made by mixing well ¼ cup of sour cream, 1 yolk of egg, 2 tablespoonfuls of sugar, ½ teaspoonful of flour, teaspoonful of lemon juice and cook it ½ minute, stirring continually. When this has cooled, stir in the beaten white of egg.

No. 60—THOUSAND PUFF TART.

1 lb. of fresh washed butter
1 lb. fine flour
½ pt. cold water
Whites of 2 eggs
2 tbsps. of rum
½ tsp. of baking powder
½ lb. of apricot or raspberry marmalade

Preparation: Mix the flour, water, egg, rum and baking powder. Cut the cold butter into bits and spread it over the dough, fold the dough over and roll out, repeat 3 to 4 times, then roll out thin. Now cut out 6 to 8 disks the size of the tart you wish to make, turn up the edge, brush over with yolks of eggs and bake light brown or yellow. Dust with sugar when done, fill in apricot or raspberry marmalade, place the disks one on top of the other. The top one should have no marmalade, but be dusted with powdered sugar.

Remarks: This tart dough can be prepared like Good Tart dough in [No. 93](), a very good recipe.

No. 61—CHEESE TART.

¼ lb. of butter

¼ lb. of sugar
½ lb. of flour
2 eggs
½ tsp. of baking powder

For the Filling.

2 lbs. of cheese
¼ lb. of butter
¼ lb. of sugar
1 tbsp. of vanilla
2 tbsps. of flour
3 eggs

Preparation: Cream the butter, add sugar, eggs, flour and baking powder. Butter a pan, roll out the dough and put in, turning up a high rim. Cheese, butter, sugar, vanilla, flour, yolks of eggs and beaten whites are mixed well, filled into the tart and baked until of a yellow color.

No. 62—APPLE TART.

½ lb. of washed butter
½ lb. of flour
¼ pt. of water
White of 1 egg
1 tbsp. of rum
¼ tsp. of baking powder

For the Filling.

1 qt. of thick apple sauce or ½ peck of apples, stewed soft in 1½ glasses of white wine and sugar

For the Frosting.

6 whites of eggs

1¼ cups of sugar
½ lb. blanched, ground almonds

Preparation: The preparation of the dough is the same as given under No. 60. The dough is rolled out, put into a buttered, round, loose bottom pan with a high rim, partly baked and spread thick with apple sauce. The 6 whites of eggs are beaten to a stiff froth, sugar and ground almonds mixed in and this frosting spread on the sauce. Now the tart is baked again to a nice light brown color.

Remarks: This tart dough can be made like Good Tart dough, in No. 93, a very good recipe.

No. 63—ORANGE TART.

8 yolks of eggs
¼ lb. of sugar almonds
Juice of 2 large oranges
¾ lb. unblanched, ground
2 tsps. of baking powder

Preparation: Yolks of eggs and sugar are stirred ½ hour, almonds and orange juice mixed in, then the baking powder and beaten whites of eggs. This dough is put into a buttered, round, loose bottom pan, strewn with bread crumbs and baked ¾ hour in medium hot oven.

No. 64—RICE TART WITH ORANGES.

¼ lb. of washed butter
½ lb. of flour
2 eggs
¼ lb. of sugar
¼ tsp. of baking powder

For the Filling.

½ lb. of rice
1 lb. of sugar
½ pt. of white wine
Juice of 1 lemon
Juice and rind of 1 orange
4 eggs

Preparation: The preparation of the dough is the same as <u>No. 61</u>. The dough is rolled out and put into the pan, making a high rim, and baked. The rice is cooked done but not mushy in 3 qts. of water. Then pour off the water, add white wine, lemon juice, orange juice, grated rind of ½ orange and sugar mixed with the rice to simmer ¼ hour. The yolks of eggs and the beaten whites are added and this mixture spread thick on the tart which is baked 20 minutes more in a medium hot oven. Instead of baking this dough, the batter may be prepared for the tart according to <u>No. 93</u>.

No. 65—BREAD TART.

12 eggs
1 lb. powdered sugar
1 pt. grated rye bread
1 tbsp. of cinnamon
1½ cups of blanched, ground almonds
1 tbsp. of citron
¼ tsp. of cardamom
1½ tsps. of baking powder

Preparation: Yolks of eggs and sugar are stirred 20 minutes, then bread, cinnamon, almonds, citron, cardamom, baking powder and beaten whites of eggs mixed in. A round, loose bottom pan is buttered, the batter filled in and the tart baked in a slow oven. You can cover the tart with a chocolate frosting.

No. 66—PUFF PASTE TART WITH CREAM.

½ lb. of washed butter
½ lb. of flour
¼ pt. of water
White of 1 egg
1 tbsp. of rum
¼ tsp. of baking powder

For the Cream.

1 pt. of cream
1½ tbsps. of flour
6 yolks of eggs
2 tbsps. of butter
Rind of ½ lemon
¼ lb. of sugar
½ cup of blanched, ground almonds

Preparation: Flour, water, egg, rum and baking powder are mixed into a dough, the butter cut into bits and spread on, the dough folded over, rolled out and this repeated several times. Cut out 3 round layers and bake them each in a round baking pan to a golden color. Meanwhile mix the cream, flour, butter, sugar, yolks of eggs, grated lemon rind and cook in double boiler to a thick cream, add the ½ cup of ground almonds, spread this cream between the layers and cover with the frosting. To make this, beat the whites of 4 eggs to a stiff froth, add 12 tablespoonfuls of sugar. After the frosting is on, put the tart into the oven again and bake to a golden yellow.

No. 67—CHERRY TART.

½ lb. of fresh butter
½ lb. of flour
¼ pt. of water
White of 1 egg
1 tbsp. of rum
¼ tsp. baking powder

For the Filling.

2 qts. of stoned cherries
1 cup of sugar

For the Frosting.

¼ lb. blanched, ground almonds
5 eggs
Sugar to taste
3 tbsps. of lemon juice

Preparation: Flour, water, egg, rum and baking powder are stirred to a dough and rolled out. The butter is cut into bits and spread on and the dough folded over and rolled out again; repeat this process 3 to 4 times and lastly put the dough into a round baking pan shaping it with a high rim. Now fill in the cherries and partly bake the cake. In the meantime prepare the frosting by mixing well 5 yolks of eggs, ground almonds, sugar, lemon juice and beaten whites of eggs. Bake the tart again to a nice color.

Remarks: This tart dough can also be made like Good Tart dough, in No. 93.

No. 68—STRAWBERRY OR RASPBERRY PUFF TART.

½ lb. of washed butter
½ lb. of flour
¼ pt. of water
White of 1 egg
1 tbsp. of rum
¼ tsp. baking powder

For the Filling.

2 qts. of strawberries
1 cup of sugar
1 qt. whipped cream

Preparation: Butter, flour, water, egg, rum and baking powder are stirred into a dough, rolled out and butter cut into bits and spread on, then folded up and rolled out again. Repeat this 3 to 4 times, cut out 3 layers which are baked to a nice color. The strawberries or raspberries are picked over, washed, mixed with sugar and whipped cream and spread between the layers. Cover with whipped cream.

No. 69—EMPEROR TART.

½ lb. blanched, roasted hazelnuts
10 eggs
½ lb. sugar
1 tsp. vanilla
2½ ozs. fine flour

For the Filling.

1 glass apricot marmalade

Preparation: The nuts are ground and stirred for ½ hour with yolks of eggs and sugar, then vanilla and flour are added and lastly the beaten whites of eggs. Bake in two layers, cool them, spread apricot marmalade between them and cover the cake with pineapple frosting.

No. 70—MOUTH POCKETS.

½ lb. of washed butter
½ lb. of flour
¼ pt. of water
¼ tsp. of baking powder
White of 1 egg
1 tbsp. of rum
Fruit marmalade

Preparation: The preparation of the dough is the same as given under No. 68. Roll out the dough very thin, cut out little tarts, put in the center of each some kind of marmalade, either raspberry, apple sauce, cherry or plum, and bake the tarts after folding one-half of each over the fruit.

No. 71—PUFF PASTE STRIPS.

½ lb. of washed butter
½ lb. of sugar
¼ pt. of water
White of 1 egg
1 tbsp. of rum
¼ tsp. baking powder
Sugar
Fruit marmalade

Preparation: The preparation of the dough is the same as given under No. 68. When the dough is rolled out thin, cut strips 3 inches long and 1½ inches wide, bake them until done, dust with sugar and finish baking. When done, spread with fruit marmalade and place two and two together.

No. 72—ALMOND TART FILLED WITH CREAM.

6 eggs
1 large cup of powdered sugar
½ lb. of unblanched, ground almonds
1½ tsps. baking powder

For the Filling.

1 pt. of whipped cream
½ cup of sugar
1 tsp. of vanilla

Preparation: Yolks of eggs and powdered sugar are beaten for 15 minutes, the ground almonds added, then the baking powder and the beaten whites of eggs.

Bake in 3 layers, cool them, then spread on whipped cream mixed with sugar and vanilla, place the layers one on the other and cover the whole cake with whipped cream. The cake may be filled with fruit marmalade.

No. 73—HUNTER'S TART.

6 eggs
½ lb. of sugar
1 grated lemon rind
1½ tsps. of baking powder
¼ lb. of fine flour

For the Filling.

Fruit marmalade or jelly

For the Frosting.

2 whites of eggs
¼ cup of sugar
2 tbsps. of lemon juice
¼ lb. blanched, ground almonds

Preparation: 4 yolks of eggs and 2 whole eggs are stirred with sugar 15 minutes, add 1 grated lemon rind, flour, baking powder, the beaten whites of 4 eggs. Butter a round, loose bottom pan, sprinkle with roll crumbs, put the batter in, and bake it in medium hot oven. When baked, spread it with marmalade and then with the frosting. This is made by beating the whites of eggs to a stiff froth and mixing it with sugar, lemon juice and almonds. Then bake the cake again in a medium hot oven until the frosting is yellow.

No. 74—FIRE TART.

7 hard-boiled eggs
½ lb. blanched, ground almonds
½ lb. sugar
Flour enough to make stiff dough

For the Filling.

Jelly or marmalade

For Sprinkling.

¼ lb. blanched, ground almonds
¼ cup of sugar

Preparation: Stir the yolks of the hard-boiled eggs well with sugar, add the almonds, then the flour, enough to make a stiff dough. Butter a pan and cover the bottom of it with dough. Leave enough for strips. Then bake the tart in a slow oven, cool it and spread it with jelly or marmalade. Mix the ground almonds with sugar and sprinkle over the jelly, then arrange the strips of dough nicely over the top and bake again. Place something under the pan that the bottom of the tart will not get dark.

No. 75—WHITE ALMOND TART.

½ lb. of butter
½ lb. of sugar
3 eggs
½ lb. of blanched, ground almonds
2½ tbsps. of baking powder
½ lb. of flour

For the Frosting.

¼ cup of rum

Powdered sugar

Preparation: Cream the butter, sugar and yolks of eggs, then add the ground almonds, the flour, the baking powder and lastly the beaten whites of eggs. Butter a round, loose bottom pan, put the batter in and bake to a nice color. The rum is mixed with enough powdered sugar to make a creamy frosting and when the tart has cooled off, spread it with this frosting.

No. 76—HEAVEN'S TART.

1 cup of fresh butter
1 cup of powdered sugar
1 egg
1 tsp. of vanilla
2 scant cups of flour
2 heaping tsps. of baking powder
3 yolks of eggs

For the Filling. No. 1.

3 whites of eggs
4 tbsps. of powdered sugar
6 bitter, ground almonds
½ tsp. of cinnamon
¼ lb. blanched, ground almonds

No. 2.

1 glass raspberry jelly

No. 3.

1 cup of cream
2 yolks of eggs
Juice of 1 lemon

1 tbsp. of flour
2 tbsps. of sugar
1 tsp. vanilla

Preparation: Cream the butter, add the sugar, egg, yolks of eggs, flour and baking powder, mix well and bake in three layers.

Beat the 3 whites of eggs to a stiff froth, add 4 tablespoonfuls of powdered sugar, ¼ lb. sweet and 6 bitter, ground almonds and vanilla, and spread on the baked layers. Put them back into the oven to bake light yellow. On two of the layers put jelly. The cup of cream, 2 yolks of eggs, lemon juice, flour, 2 tablespoonfuls of sugar and 1 teaspoonful of vanilla are mixed well and boiled to a cream, stirring constantly. Let it get cold, spread it over the two layers covered with jelly and place one on the other. Place the layers covered with the beaten whites of eggs on top.

No. 77—HEAVEN'S FOOD.

2 eggs
1 cup of sugar
2 heaping tbsps. of flour
1 tsp. of baking powder
½ cup of ground walnuts
½ cup of chopped dates

For the Filling.

3 oranges
1 pt. of whipped cream
2 bananas

Preparation: The eggs are well-beaten and stirred with sugar for 10 minutes; add flour and baking powder, ground walnuts and chopped dates and bake the cake to a nice color. When it is done, break it in desirable pieces, place them close together again, put the sliced oranges and bananas on and cover the whole with whipped cream mixed with sugar and vanilla. Serve at once.

No. 78—MERINGUE TART.

6 whites of eggs
2 cups of sugar
1 tsp. of vanilla
¼ tsp. of cream of tartar
1 tbsp. of vinegar

Preparation: The whites of eggs must be beaten very stiff, the cream of tartar, sugar and vanilla added and beaten or stirred 1 hour. Rinse a round cake pan with water, put the mixture in and bake in a slow oven 1 hour. When cold, fill it with whipped cream.

No. 79—SPONGE CAKE.

4 eggs
1 cup of sugar
3 tbsps. of water
1 cup of sifted flour
1 pinch of salt
1 tsp. of vanilla or lemon
1 tsp. of baking powder

Preparation: Cream the yolks of eggs and sugar, add the flour, water, salt and vanilla, then add baking powder and beaten whites of eggs. Butter a pan, put the batter in and bake slowly.

No. 80—WALNUT TART.

7 eggs
2 cups of powdered sugar
Juice of 1 lemon
½ cup of dates
2½ tsps. of baking powder
½ cup of sifted cracker crumbs
¾ lb. of blanched walnuts

Preparation: Rub yolks of eggs to a cream with sugar, add the ground walnuts, chopped dates, lemon juice, cracker crumbs, baking powder and beaten whites of eggs. Butter a round, loose bottom cake pan, put the batter in, bake it to a nice color, and cover with a chocolate frosting.

No. 81—BISCUIT TART.

12 eggs
1 lb. of sugar
1¼ tsps. baking powder
1 tsp. of vanilla or lemon rind
11 ozs. of flour

Preparation: Cream the yolks of eggs and sugar, add vanilla or grated ½ lemon rind, flour, baking powder and the beaten whites of eggs. Butter a round, loose bottom pan, put the batter in and bake in a slow oven. A glass of fine wine poured over the baked tart makes it very nice.

No. 82—SAND TART.

1 lb. of butter
10 eggs 1 lb.
1 lb. of sugar
The juice and rind of 1 lemon
2 tbsps. of good brandy
1 lb. corn starch or half corn starch and half flour

1 tsp. of baking powder

Preparation: The butter is washed to take the salt out, then creamed; add gradually the sugar and yolks of eggs, lemon juice, grated lemon rind and brandy. Then add the flour in spoonfuls. All in all the batter must have been stirred 1 hour. Now add the baking powder and beaten whites of eggs. Butter a round, loose bottom pan, put the batter in and bake slowly 1½ hours.

No. 83—FILLED BISCUIT ROLLS.

4 eggs
¼ lb. of sugar
1 tsp. grated lemon rind
¼ lb. of flour
1 tbsp. of butter
1 cup of fruit marmalade

Preparation: The yolks of eggs and sugar are stirred ½ hour, then the grated lemon rind, flour and beaten whites of eggs mixed in. A pan is buttered with the 1 tablespoonful of butter, the batter spread in ¼ inch thick and baked in a medium hot oven to a light brown color. When still warm, spread with the marmalade, roll it up and cut slices of it which may be baked or dried a little in the oven. If you wish, cover them with frosting.

No. 84—DATE CAKE WITH WHIPPED CREAM.

6 eggs
½ lb. of sugar
½ lb. of chopped walnuts
1 lb. chopped dates
½ cup of wheat bread crumbs
2 tsps. of baking powder

For the Filling.

1 pt. of whipped cream

Preparation: The yolks of eggs are creamed with sugar, then add the chopped or ground walnuts and dates, bread crumbs, baking powder and beaten whites of eggs. Bake in 2 layers. Mix the whipped cream with sugar and ½ teaspoonful of vanilla, spread on the layers and arrange these one on the other. Serve at once.

No. 85—FARINA TART.

7 eggs
¾ cup of sugar
½ cup blanched, ground, sweet almonds
15 bitter, blanched, ground almonds
1 grated lemon peel
¼ lb. of farina, good measure

Preparation: The yolks of eggs, sugar, lemon peel and almonds are stirred 1 hour, the farina mixed in dry and lastly the beaten whites of eggs. Butter a round, loose bottom pan, put the batter in and bake slowly 1 hour.

No. 86—BROWN SPICE CAKE No. 3.

2 cups of brown sugar
1 cup of butter
3 eggs
1 cup of milk
3 cups of flour
1 tsp. of cloves
½ tsp. of nutmeg
1 cup of chopped raisins
1 cup of chopped hickory nuts

3 tsps. of baking powder
1 tsp. of cinnamon

Preparation: Cream the butter with sugar and yolks of eggs, add the milk, cloves, cinnamon, nutmeg, raisins, nuts, flour, baking powder and whites of eggs. Butter a pan, put the batter in and bake 1¼ to 1½ hours in medium hot oven.

No. 87—SPICE CAKE No. 4.

½ cup of butter
½ cup of lard
1½ cups of dark brown sugar
2 eggs
½ cup of cold coffee
½ cup of sour milk
1 tsp. of soda
¾ tsp. of cinnamon
½ tsp. cloves
3½–4 cups of flour

Preparation: The butter, lard, yolks of eggs and sugar are stirred to a cream, add the coffee, sour milk in which the soda has been dissolved, cinnamon, cloves, flour and beaten whites of eggs. Butter a pan, put the batter in and bake 1 hour or bake in 3 layers.

No. 88—SCOTCH TART.

¾ lb. of butter
1 lb. of sugar
½ lb. of finely cut raisins
9 eggs
Juice and rind of 1 lemon
1 lb. of flour

2 heaping tsps. of baking powder

Preparation: The butter is stirred to a cream, with yolks of eggs, sugar, lemon juice and rind; add the flour and lastly the baking powder and beaten whites of eggs. Butter a pan, put the batter in and bake to a light brown color.

No. 89—LARD CAKE.

½ lb. pork lard
6 eggs
½ lb. of sugar
¼ lb. of corn starch
¼ lb. of flour
½ lb. blanched, ground, sweet almonds
20 blanched, ground, bitter almonds
1 heaping tsp. of baking powder

Preparation: Stir the yolks of eggs and sugar to a cream; cream the lard and mix with the eggs and sugar. Now add flour and almonds in spoonfuls and lastly the baking powder and beaten whites of eggs. Butter a pan, put the batter in and bake to a nice brown color.

No. 90—SEXTON'S CAKE.

½ lb. of butter
¼ lb. of sugar
½ lb. of extra fine flour
¼ lb. blanched, ground, sweet almonds
½ tsp. baking powder

Preparation: The butter is stirred to a cream; add the sugar, ground almonds, flour and baking powder and stir 45 minutes. Spread the batter ½ inch thick in small square muffin pans or in a large square buttered cake pan, bake it to a light brown color and leave it to cool a little before taking out of the pan, because it breaks easily. After it has cooled off completely, dust with sugar or spread frosting on.

No. 91—CHOCOLATE TART.

¼ lb. sweet chocolate
1 cup of water
¼ lb. ground almonds
¼ lb. of butter
3 eggs
1¼ cups of sugar
1½ tsps. of baking powder
2 cups of flour

For Filling.

1 pt. of whipped cream

Preparation: Stir the butter, sugar and yolks of eggs to a cream. Add the chocolate dissolved in water, unblanched, ground almonds, flour and baking powder and the beaten whites of eggs. Butter a round, loose bottom pan, put the batter in and bake in a slow oven. Mix the whipped cream with sugar and vanilla and fill or cover the tart with it before serving.

No. 92—ENGLISH BRIDE'S CAKE (FRUIT CAKE).

1 lb. of butter
1 lb. brown sugar
10 eggs
1 lb. of flour
1 pt. of brandy
1 tbsp. ground cinnamon
2 lbs. finely cut citron

½ tbsp. of ground cloves
4 ground nutmegs
1 tsp. of baking soda
1 cup of molasses
10 lbs. of raisins
4 lbs. of currants
1 tbsp. of ground bark of nutmeg

Preparation: The butter is stirred to a cream with sugar and yolks of eggs. Then work in ½ lb. of flour, the brandy mixed with the spices and the molasses in which the soda is dissolved, the beaten whites of eggs, then raisins, currants, citron and the other ½ lb. of flour. The cake is baked 3 to 4 hours.

Remarks: This cake may be kept 20 years and longer and will still be palatable. Wine is served with it.

No. 93—GOOD TART DOUGH.

¼ lb. of butter
2 yolks of eggs
¼ lb. of blanched, ground almonds
¼ lb. of sugar
1 tbsp. of brandy
2 cups of flour
½ cup of cracker crumbs

Preparation: Cream the butter with sugar, egg yolks and brandy, and add the flour. Roll out the dough and line a round, loose bottom pan with it. Strew with ½ cup of cracker crumbs and ¼ lb. blanched, ground almonds. Spread the fruit on the almonds. This dough is very good for any kind of Fruit Tart.

No. 94—CHOCOLATE TART No. 2.

6 eggs
1 cup sugar
⅛ lb. chopped bitter chocolate
20 chopped almonds
½ cup of flour
1 heaping tsp. of baking powder

For Filling.

1 pt. of whipped cream

Preparation: Beat the whites of eggs to a stiff froth, add the chopped bitter chocolate and almonds, then yolks of eggs and sugar, and lastly the flour and baking powder. Bake in two layers. A little before serving, spread whipped cream between the layers.

No. 95—FILLED SAND TART.

Sand tart batter as in No. 82.

For Filling.

1 glass of fine fruit marmalade

For Frosting.

Rum frosting according to Chapter 20, No. 22

Preparation: The sand tart batter should be baked in 3 layers; when cold, spread the fruit marmalade between the layers. Then cover with rum frosting.

No. 96—TREE TART.

7 eggs
1 cup sugar

1 cup finest flour
Chocolate or sour filling

Preparation: Beat the yolks with a rotary egg beater, add ½ cup sugar and beat well again, then set aside. Beat whites to stiff froth, add other ½ cup sugar. Mix both and add 1 cup flour measured before sifting. Butter pans, dredge them with flour and put the batter in. Bake in 8 layers in a slow oven. Spread chocolate or sour cream filling as in No. 76, between the layers. You may also cover with a frosting if you wish.

No. 97—FENCE TART.

First Layer.

4 whites of eggs
3 yolks of egg
1 pinch of salt
⅓ tsp. cream of tartar
1¼ cups of sugar
1 cup flour

Second Layer.

⅓ or ¼ lb. bitter chocolate dissolved in ¼ cup hot water
1 cup of powdered sugar
1 tsp. of vanilla
½ package Knox gelatine dissolved in ¼ cup of water
1½ cups of cream
½ pt. whipped cream

Third Layer.

½ package Knox gelatine with pink coloring dissolved in ¼ cup of water
1 cup of powdered sugar
1½ cups of cream
½ pt. whipped cream

1 tsp. of vanilla

For the Covering.

1 pt. whipped cream

For the Fencing.

1½ doz, ladyfingers or macaroons

Preparation: The first layer. Whip whites of eggs to thin froth, add salt and cream of tartar, then whip to a stiff froth, mix in the sugar and then the yolks of eggs whipped to a cream. Mix the flour in lightly and bake this batter in a buttered, round, loose bottom pan. Loosen edge of layer and arrange ladyfingers or macaroons around in circle. For the second layer. The dissolved bitter chocolate, sugar, cream and vanilla are boiled for 2 minutes, stirring constantly; stir in the dissolved gelatine, set the mixture in cold water and continue stirring until it begins to thicken, then add the ½ pint of whipped cream and spread the mixture over the baked layer. The third layer is made exactly like the second layer only using the pink coloring instead of the bitter chocolate; after the whipped cream is added, spread the mixture over the chocolate layer.

Before serving, spread the 1 pint of whipped cream, to which has been added a little sugar and vanilla, over the cake.

No. 98—FRUIT TART.

Apricot, Peach, Plum, Blueberry, Raspberry or Strawberry Tart.

Prepare the batter according to [No. 93](), Good Tart Dough. Cover with the desired fruit, either fresh or canned, sprinkle with sufficient sugar, bake for 25 minutes. Before serving the cake, cover with beaten cream or almond frosting, prepared according to [No. 23](), Chapter 20 and then bake.

No. 99—SUNSHINE CAKE.

6 eggs
1 cup sugar
1 cup flour
1 even tsp. cream of tartar
Pinch of salt
½ tsp. vanilla

Preparation: Beat the yolks of eggs first and add half the sugar; beat the whites of eggs very dry and add remaining sugar; beat well and add the vanilla, salt and the yolks of eggs; lastly, add the flour and cream of tartar. Bake in a moderate oven one hour.

No. 100—LOVE CHOCOLATE CAKE.

¼ cup butter
1 cup sugar
1 egg
1 tsp. vanilla
½ cup sour milk
½ tsp. soda
2 squares bitter chocolate
½ cup hot water
1 large cup flour

Preparation: Cream butter and sugar; add the egg and vanilla; add the milk in which the soda is dissolved; dissolve the chocolate in a half cup boiling water, let cool and add; lastly, add the flour. Bake in flat cake tin about 45 minutes.

No. 101—ANGEL FOOD.

Whites of 9 eggs
1 cup sugar
1 tsp. vanilla
1 cup flour
1 tsp. cream of tartar

Preparation: Beat the whites of eggs to a stiff froth; boil the sugar with 4 tablespoons of water until all the sugar is dissolved; beat the sugar syrup into the whites of the eggs; add vanilla and the flour and cream of tartar. Bake slowly one hour.

No. 102—FRUIT CAKE.

1¼ cups sugar
½ cup butter
Yolks of 2 eggs
1 cup sour milk
1 tsp. baking soda
1½ cups flour
½ tsp. cloves
½ tsp. cinnamon
½ cup dates, raisins and citron
1 cup walnuts

Preparation: Cream the sugar and butter, add yolks of eggs, cloves and cinnamon; dissolve the soda in the sour milk and add to the rest; add the flour and mix well; lastly add the raisins, dates, citron and walnuts. Bake about 45 minutes.

No. 103—CREAM PUFFS.

1 large teacup hot water

½ tsp. butter
1 teacup flour
4 eggs

Preparation: Stir the flour into the boiling water and butter. Set aside to cool and, when cold, stir in the unbeaten eggs one at a time. Drop in muffin tins and bake in a fairly hot oven. When baked, fill with beaten cream, sweetened to taste and flavored with vanilla.

No. 104—CREAM PUFFS.

1 cup boiling water
½ cup butter
1 cup pastry flour
3 eggs, beaten
Small pinch of soda

Preparation; Pour the water over the butter. As soon as it boils and the butter is melted, stir in the flour and keep stirring until it leaves the sides of the pan. Let cool, stir in the eggs and soda, drop on the buttered pans and bake thirty minutes. Do not open the oven door for twenty minutes for fear they will fall. Fill with whipped cream, sweetened and flavored.

No. 105—YEAST DOUGHNUTS.

1 cup sugar
3 cups milk
Flour to make soft sponge
1 yeast cake
Mix and let stand over night

In the Morning Add:

1 cup sugar

½ cup butter
3 eggs
½ a nutmeg
½ tsp. soda
Flour to mix stiff

Preparation: Let rise, then roll and cut in shape desired, or roll into long strips and twist into shape. Let rise again while the lard is heating and then fry. Raised doughnuts require longer cooking.

No. 106—SOUR CREAM DOUGHNUTS.

5 tbsps. sour cream
1 cup milk
½ cup butter
2 eggs
Little salt
1 tsp. soda
¼ tsp. cinnamon
¼ tsp. nutmeg
1 tsp. baking powder
1 cup sugar
1¼ pts. of flour

Preparation: Stir butter, eggs and cream well, add all other ingredients, roll and cut the dough, bake in hot lard to golden brown color and sprinkle powdered sugar over.

No. 107—BLITZ-KUCHEN.

1 lb. sugar
½ lb. butter
8 eggs
1 lb. flour

Preparation: Stir sugar, butter and yolks of eggs together well, add the stiffly beaten whites of eggs and flour. Bake in a long tin and cover with sugar, cinnamon and chopped almonds. Cut and serve while warm.

No. 108—SPICE CAKE.

2 cups brown sugar
½ cup butter
2 eggs
2 egg yolks
½ cup sour milk
1 tsp. nutmeg
2 cups flour
1 tsp. cloves
1 tsp. cinnamon
1 tsp. soda

Preparation: Beat the sugar, butter and eggs together until smooth; add the remaining ingredients. Bake in three layers and put together with white frosting.

No. 109—WHIPPED CREAM CAKE.

Make a good sponge cake dough (see No. 29). and omit the chocolate.

Filling.

1 pint whipped, sweet cream
1 pound blanched, chopped almonds
Vanilla
Sugar

Preparation: After the layers are baked, beat the cream stiff, add sugar, vanilla and almonds; sweeten the cream and spread between the layers and on top. This is the queen of all cakes.

No. 110—WALNUT CAKE.

1 lb. walnuts (leave out 14 halves for the top)
1 cup powdered sugar
¾ cup crackers (rolled fine)
8 eggs
1 tsp. baking powder
1 cup powdered sugar

Filling.

2 cups milk
Corn starch to thicken
½ cup sugar
Vanilla
Yolks of 2 eggs

Preparation: Cream the yolks of eggs and the sugar; add the beaten whites of the eggs; mix the rolled crackers, finely chopped nuts and baking powder and add. Bake in three layers in a slow oven.

Stir powdered sugar with a little water, spread on top of cake and put on the walnut halves.

No. 111—ANGEL CAKE.

1 scant cup flour
1 scant cup sugar
1 tsp. baking powder
1 cup walnuts (cut)
1 cup dates (cut)
4 eggs

Preparation: Cream the eggs separately, add sugar, walnuts, dates, baking powder and flour. Bake in a buttered pan.